PRAISE FOR

Happy to Help

"In this honest, insightful, and often hilarious account, Amy Wilson explores her experience and frustrations as a people pleaser. Her story will resonate with anyone who has said 'Happy to help!' one too many times. I couldn't put it down."

—GRETCHEN RUBIN,
author of *The Happiness Project*

"My fellow type-A souls, Amy Wilson understands us. It's time to put down all we've been carrying, pick up this funny, all-too-relatable memoir, and rejoice in the empathy of a kindred spirit. Let someone else run the world today."

—MARY LAURA PHILPOTT,
author of *I Miss You When I Blink*

"A gift to women everywhere. This book is not just a critique of contemporary culture; it is a beacon of hope and guidance. With thought-provoking insights and practical wisdom, Wilson provides readers with the tools to navigate the tricky path out of our modern-day achievement trap."

—JENNIFER BREHENY WALLACE,
author of *Never Enough: When Achievement Culture Becomes Toxic—and What We Can Do About It*

"Funny, wise, and delightful—and smart and reassuring—*Happy to Help* will have you caught between laughing and nodding along, and maybe dropping a few balls you've been keeping in the air to give you time to read one more page."

—KJ DELL'ANTONIA,
author of *How to Be a Happier Parent*

"Amy Wilson is the wise and good-humored companion we all deserve in our lives. Her writing strikes an insightful balance between lighthearted and soul-searching, reassuring us that we're not alone in wondering where all the grownups have gone, leaving us—us??—to make The Big Decisions."

—REBECCA N. THOMPSON, MD,
author of *Held Together: A Shared Memoir of Motherhood, Medicine, and Imperfect Love*

"Wilson's refreshing and hilarious essays illustrate the ridiculous nature of the advice meant to fix women, and the unfair emotional labor expectations we place on them. *Happy to Help* offers a new narrative that inspires women to hold true boundaries and value their time as diamonds. A must-read!"

—EVE RODSKY,
author of *Fair Play*

Happy to Help

ALSO BY AMY WILSON

*When Did I Get Like This?: The Screamer, the Worrier,
the Dinosaur-Chicken-Nugget Buyer,
& Other Mothers I Swore I'd Never Be*

Happy to Help

ADVENTURES OF A PEOPLE PLEASER

Amy Wilson

ZIBBY BOOKS
NEW YORK

Happy to Help: Adventures of a People Pleaser

Copyright © 2025 by Amy Wilson

All rights reserved. No part of this book may be used, reproduced, distributed, or transmitted in any form or by any means without the prior written permission of the publisher, except as permitted by U.S. copyright law. Published in the United States by Zibby Books LLC, New York.

Zibby Books, colophon, and associated logos are trademarks and/or registered trademarks of Zibby Media LLC.

The author has tried to re-create events, locales, and conversations based on their own memories and those of others. In some instances, in order to maintain their anonymity, certain names, characteristics, and locations have been changed.

"The Oldest Sister" © Lois Duncan from *Seasons of the Heart* (iUniverse, 2007). Used by permission.

Library of Congress Control Number: 2024933056
Paperback ISBN: 978-1-958506-78-3
Hardcover ISBN: 978-1-958506-79-0
eBook ISBN: 978-1-958506-80-6

Book design by Neuwirth & Associates
Cover design by Abby Weintraub

www.zibbymedia.com

Printed in the United States of America

10 9 8 7 6 5 4 3 2 1

*for Nancy
and for Maggie*

Be still sometimes.
Be still sometimes.
Let it all fall sometimes.

—Rose Cook,
"A Poem for Someone Who is Juggling Her Life"

AUTHOR'S NOTE

The experiences and events recalled in this book are true. My recollections are based on my perceptions and memories of those events, and I have done my best to portray those events as accurately as possible.

Some names and identifying details of people and places have been changed in order to protect the privacy of others.

Contents

Introduction	1
Give It All You've Got	9
Stop Before It's Too Much	15
You Were Made for This	23
Know Your Value	29
Do What Matters	45
The Truth Will Set You Free	59
The Only One You Can Change Is You	75
Never Give Up	89
First, Do No Harm	105
Make New Friends, but Keep the Old	123
Sometimes You Just Have to Laugh	137
Keep the Faith	147
We're All in This Together	161
No Hard Feelings	179
Look on the Bright Side	201
It's Never Too Late	215
Cherish Every Moment	223
It Has to Be You	239
Notes on Sources	253
Acknowledgments	257

Introduction

If you've picked up this book, you are probably someone with a lot to do. Perhaps a little *too* much. When you mention this to others, they may respond that what you really need to do is less.

Just let go! Stop doing so much!

They make it sound like it's easy.

Perhaps for those people it is easy.

I am not one of those people.

When my children were little, I took somewhat excessive pride in navigating New York City as one grown-up managing all three: my baby in a sling, three-year-old in the stroller, four-year-old riding the jerry-rigged running board just behind. Underneath the stroller was a diaper bag so thoroughly stocked with everything we might need that it felt magical to me, even though I was the one who had packed it.

On weekday mornings we would all take the city bus to my sons' preschool drop-off. As the bus pulled up at our stop, I would feel the presumptive annoyance of those behind us in line, sure that our getting on ahead of them would take all day, at least until they saw me in action: boarding the boys one at a time, pulling our MetroCard from a dedicated side pocket, and folding the stroller in a highly practiced one-handed snap. I wanted to win the bus stop line so completely that the people behind me would show up at work and announce, "My God, you wouldn't *believe* how capable a woman I just saw on the M104."

Maybe that happened at some point. I'll never know. I wasn't handing out business cards or anything. (The one thing I never thought to pack in that diaper bag.)

At the same time, though, I yearned for something else. I wanted someone to approach my young family, as we scored a cumulative 9.8 in Bus Boarding, and say, "Look at you, with all those kids! Let me hold the stroller for a second. Let me grab that bag. Let me *help* you." If I couldn't get a medal on 91st and Broadway, I was at least hoping for a little assistance. But no one ever told me they noticed all that I was managing, and that I was really good at it. And why would anyone have offered me help, when I was endeavoring so hard to show everyone that I didn't need any?

And so I see you. You look like you have your act together. Hell, you *do*. But you've got way too much on your plate. You're waiting for someone, anyone, to notice and say, "Hey, let me carry some of that."

Instead, they say, "Why don't you try carrying less?"

Or, "Hey, I think you dropped something."

And they're so right, they're so exactly right. You cannot handle it all. You have to let some of it go. But then you look at all the things you're carrying, and you wonder what exactly it is you're supposed to put down when the answer feels like nothing.

I'm here to tell you that you're right too.

You do a lot. (*Somebody* has to.) A lot of it is for other people.

Introduction

And when no one else is helping, you help more, and brighter, and faster. It's not that no one ever expresses their gratitude for all that you do. Their greeting-card sentiments are lovely: they just don't know what they'd do without you! But that is, of course, meant as a compliment. Not to be taken literally. Not as an expression of actual concern that you would ever stop showing up. You are the one who can be counted on. You are happy to help. And that is why everyone but you is content with the way things are, you doing your share and half of theirs as well.

The real question might be why some of us are like this, having taken on way more to do than we can handle, and how it all became ours to do in the first place. On that front, I might be the last person you should look to for advice. I have suffered from the curse of capability all my life, way before I became a mother and a writer and a performer and the pancake breakfast co-chair. The truth is, I have overdelivered ever since I was an eight-year-old taking the Brownie pledge:

> *On my honor, I will try:*
> *To serve God and my country,*
> *To help people at all times,*
> *And to live by the Girl Scout Law.*

Help people *at all times*? That's a rather global undertaking for a second-grader. But for me, a Scout in knee socks saluting the flag, it was a clarion call. And ever since then, when given an assignment—no matter how thankless or voluntary—I have always done my best to see it through. And then some. After all, you get extra points when you put others first. You might be uncomfortable, but you also get to be good.

It's not like people like us start out intending to carry *everything*. The overwhelm happens a little at a time. One minute you're canvassing your neighborhood selling Girl Scout cookies; the next minute you're the valedictorian or drum majorette—or both. Then in a blink you're the default parent, ringmaster of obligations for your spouse and kids. And all the other organizations we exist within, whether they're law firms or preschool auction committees, truly believe that we, the identified capable ones, really are the best candidates for completing this one more tiny thing (when we have a chance). We say yes to each task as it's added to our list, getting ever further from the end of what there is to do, and we figure we are supposed to keep bailing water until someone else grabs the bucket. Sometimes that happens. Other times everyone else abandons ship while we keep at it, the last ones to see that no matter how hard we work, the boat we are in will continue to slowly sink.

Not that it always turns out that badly. And it's not that we mind being in charge, because things usually go pretty well when we are. Plus, if everyone's letting us be in control, that must be because we're pretty good at it.

This is comforting. It's also unsustainable.

Eventually all of us reach a breaking point. And at moments in my life when I have admitted that I was overwhelmed and asked for help, there were definitely times I have gotten assistance. There were other times that I've received, instead of help, an explanation that I had brought this all on myself. That I never should have been doing so much in the first place.

But when I look back at my life, through adolescence and career and mothering and living, the improbable goals I set for myself were not ones I dreamed up. They were achievements I

Introduction

was told I should want, assignments I printed out for my internal Trapper Keeper of expectations and held tightly to my chest. Yes, I've sometimes sought my sense of purpose in other people. The boundaries where I stop and others begin have not always been so clear. But I'm a woman, and they're not supposed to be. We are supposed to do a lot of caretaking, and we are not supposed to make a big deal about it. And if you're like me, having revealed even the tiniest inclination toward being dependable and good at getting things done, you can end up feeling like the power lines on the side of the road, always just there making things happen, so reliably that people quickly stop processing their presence.

Or never really notice them in the first place.

There are people who are nothing like us, of course. There are people—and, yes, some are women—who ignore the sign-up sheets, who are indifferent to what they see in the mirror, who stay in bed as long as they like in the mornings without wondering if anyone else let the dog out. (They have not.) These are the sort of people who pride themselves on "going with the flow" without wondering just who might be creating said flow. "I wish I were as strong as those women," a guest on my podcast told me recently, apologizing that she needed to end our interview a bit early so she could run and do something for her kid's school. This was someone who'd written multiple books, raised three kids, started two businesses, negotiated a divorce and a remarriage and a blended family, deeming herself weaker than others who might do less. "I wish I could be like that," she said, imagining herself as someone able to ignore the request that she volunteer to make her son's school better. The sort of person nobody expected to help in the first place.

I understood this woman's disappointment in her own reliability. I understood why she envied those who know how to sit back. But opting out isn't as easy as it sounds. What is it exactly that you can hand over when the same loving partner who wishes you "could just relax sometimes"—and who is probably not wrong for saying so—wants that evolution to come at zero cost to their own spare time? When the foundation of your childhood home is crumbling and you're the only sibling who lives nearby? When you ask if anyone else might want to take over Toys for Tots this year, and absolutely no one does, because everyone else in town has an ounce of sense?

Some books will tell you that your expectations are too high. Your micromanagement and gatekeeping are running the show, and that's no fun for anyone. Just go with the flow! Other books will say you're imagining things; that wall you're banging your head against would crumble if you could only understand, small lovely one, that you *are* the wall. If you let go of your heavy burdens, they might just float away, free of your leaden expectations, balloons now making for the open sky. Others will tell you that you are powerful beyond measure and can accomplish much more than you believe. Relief will come when you get out of your own way. You only *think* you don't have enough time. Work harder. Change faster.

Still others will tell you that you shouldn't have picked up all that heavy stuff in the first place. I mean, touché, but when you try to redistribute, no one else wants any of it. Maybe because they read those other books sooner.

Introduction

So then what? You could drop it all, but then some of it might break. You could leave it in the road, but then it would just be sitting there, and you'd hate for anyone to think you're a litterbug.

While the assignments the world gives us as women are many, our choices are few. When we say that we have more to do than we can handle, we are often told that we're perfectionists, or workaholics, or not *letting* people help us, or just making things harder than they need to be—none of which is very helpful. When we set out to fix our own people pleasing or inefficiency, instead of our problems, we're taking on even more assignments. We're giving ourselves no grace at all when grace may be the thing most required.

So, yes, you do have to let some of this go. But what should go first is the idea that there's something wrong with you. Whatever you're currently managing? It really is as hard as you think it is. What you have on your plate is objectively insane, and you don't have to convince me. I'm tipping my hat to you as I write these words. (Or I would be, if my own hands weren't so full.)

The world might think that people who see what needs to be done, and then try to help accomplish it, can be sort of annoying. It might roll its eyes at us for allowing ourselves to be so overextended. Then it will ask us if we had any thoughts about dinner. Then it will email us a reminder for the fundraising kickoff call next Wednesday evening. The world may resent us for being extra, but that doesn't mean it wants us to quit.

And so maybe we do need to look to ourselves first. If we are to accept that what we're doing is too much, making a change requires an exploration of how we got here. This book is about the times I have done too much and what happened when I tried to do things differently. It's about the times I've tried to finish what I started, and then tried harder. It's about the ways we're all told we're weak, or sick, or crazy, or wrong when we say that what we have to do is more than we can handle.

And it's about the advice we receive whenever we ask for help, express doubt about what we can accomplish, or try to push back on the way things are. Sometimes, in the end, that advice has actually worked for me. Usually, it definitely didn't.

This isn't a book about foolproof ways to get other people to step up. This isn't a book that offers step-by-step instructions on how to stop giving a crap. And it's definitely not about how to do less. That part, for me, is still in progress. But this book does offer recognition that we are, most of us, managing quite a lot, and doing just fine. And if we have created our too-long lists one unset boundary at a time, learning a new path might take just as long.

As Lao Tzu once said, "By letting go, it all gets done."

Well: no, it doesn't. But maybe that's okay too.

Give It All You've Got

At some point in the winter of my eighth-grade year I decided to stop raising my hand in class. I had newly sensed the resentment of some of my classmates that I was always ready with an answer. Up until then I had been rather eager to share my intelligence with the group, but now the boys in the eighth grade had taken to calling me "Brainiac," and although everyone said boys teased you only because they liked you, this did not feel like an expression of fondness. "Brainiac" was not a name for a girl boys liked. "Brainiac" sounded like a too-smart, no-personality robot programmed without the human capability of reading the room.

The solution was obvious. I would stop raising my hand.

The first class I attended as this new-and-improved me was English with Sister Benedicta, who at sixty-seven years old seemed ancient to me. That year marked Sister Benedicta's fortieth anniversary of corralling thirteen-year-olds into sitting up straight and diagramming sentences. Sister Benedicta had made it her life's work to wage war on middle schoolers' split infinitives, although I'm not sure why; it was clear to all of us at St. Paul School in Scranton, Pennsylvania, that eighth graders were utmost in Sister Benedicta's hierarchy of disdain.

As class president of 8 Blue, I had been determined to change that. I would get Sister Benedicta to like us. After gaining intel that it would soon be her birthday, I surreptitiously collected three dollars from each of my classmates during homeroom. I opened the phone book to choose a florist, then decided a bouquet of balloons was an even better choice. Even Sister Benedicta's spirits would be lifted by balloons! Or so I thought, until those balloons were delivered in the middle of homeroom by someone in a gorilla costume, an added bit of flair I had definitely not specified.

No one dared laugh. Even the boys in the back row knew someone's head was going to roll for the extreme blasphemy of inviting a gorilla into such a hallowed place of learning as 8 Blue. I found it hard to breathe. But Sister Benedicta was more bewildered than angry, her mouth a tight line as she asked just exactly whose idea this had been. When I confessed, she did not send me to the principal for immediate expulsion, but did chastise me for spending money on something so unnecessary when we could have just made a donation to the missionaries abroad in her honor. In hindsight, that did seem like something she might have enjoyed more.

The day I decided to stop raising my hand, Sister Benedicta was at the blackboard introducing the declension of the verb "to skate." Learning English back then, at least as the Sisters of the Immaculate Heart of Mary taught it, meant accessing grammar through memorization of its many nested subcategories. Verbs could be perfect and subjunctive and indicative and imperative. Much of it was baffling to my classmates, but its orderliness spoke to me. Know the rules, and then you knew everything. Even when things became complicated.

"Who can decline this verb in the future perfect continuous tense?" Sister Benedicta asked.

It was easy. You just took the regular future continuous tense, then dropped the perfect part into the middle. *I shall have been skating. You will have been skating. He or she will have been skating.*

"Anyone?" Sister Benedicta said.

The hard part was not raising my hand. But I wanted my classmates to like me more than I wanted to be the one with the answer.

"Does anyone know the future perfect continuous?"

My eyes darted to Diep Tran, the only other kid who might have a clue. I could tell even she had no idea.

Sister Benedicta stood at her lectern. The silence became uneasy.

"And you, Amy?" Sister Benedicta turned to me with an eyebrow raised. "Do you know the future perfect continuous, in the first person?"

"I . . . shall have been skating?" I hoped I sounded sufficiently uncertain.

Sister Benedicta nodded. "So you did know. You knew the answer."

"Yes, Sister."

"But you chose not to share it."

I couldn't tell where Sister Benedicta was going with this. Was she simply seeking clarification? I decided to stick with the basics. "Yes, Sister."

Two red splotches suddenly graced Sister Benedicta's cheeks. "Do you think you're better than everyone else here?"

I froze. I had opted out of raising my hand so my classmates wouldn't think that about me. Now Sister Benedicta was drawing that conclusion on their behalf.

"Do you? Do you think you're better than your classmates? Please. Tell us."

Blood pounded in my ears. I was afraid to answer, and more afraid not to. "No, Sister."

Sister Benedicta nodded, as if she had known I would say that, as if I had only confirmed her disappointment. "Then how dare you?" she asked. "How dare you withhold information that others might find useful?"

I had nothing to say in response. I was mortified that I had disappointed her, mortified also that my classmates might join her in these feelings of scorn.

From that, at least, I was spared: everyone in 8 Blue was as unsettled by Sister Benedicta's outburst as I was. If "Brainiac" was getting yelled at, absolutely no one was safe.

How dare I?

Sister Benedicta's unanswered question hung there for the rest of the year, tacitly withdrawn but still visible, like last week's spelling words on the chalkboard.

I've thought of Sister Benedicta's anger many times in the decades since, searching for just what it was I did that made her so full of indignation. But the older I get, the less I understand it. Sometimes I think her outburst had nothing to do with me: it was just a moment of displaced frustration, of suppressed rage, exhibited by someone who had taken a lifelong vow of obedience at eighteen. If it hadn't been me, it would have been one of my classmates soon enough—probably one of the boys in the back row, far more accustomed to her ire, far more able to snicker and shrug it off as soon as the bell rang. At other times I think that it was exactly about me—that what made Sister Benedicta so angry was looking at a girl in the fast-forward stages of her adolescence who was making, for the very first time, the choice to shrink herself and become something less.

Whatever her actual motivation may have been, what Sister Benedicta corrected in me that day was the notion that I could ever slack off. I could not hang back, not even if others didn't like it, not even if *I* didn't like it.

I was obliged to share, with whomever might ask, everything I had to give.

Maybe that was the day I became the person who really doesn't mind taking notes during meetings, the one who's pretty sure she saved that form, the one with a safety pin somewhere in the bottom of her backpack.

Or maybe I was born destined to have a to-do list that only gets longer, never shorter, despite my constant efforts to Get It All Done once and for all. *Call the pharmacy. Figure out what the kids are doing next summer. Check the portal. Prep the agenda. Listen to those voicemails. Fill out that form.*

Figure out where I put that form, then *fill it out.*

There's another, interior list of things I tell myself whenever I engage with my inventory of assignments: *This is insane! I can't do all of this! What was I thinking?* I can't get anything done because

I am too angry at myself for having so much to do in the first place.

To get out of that funk, I will further procrastinate by giving myself a pep talk, telling myself I am doing my best. That I just have to get through this next week, or season, or deadline, or developmental stage, and that things will most certainly slow down after that, because next time I will know my limits.

Next time I will know better.

Won't I?

Stop Before It's Too Much

In the second summer of the pandemic—a time when I and every other woman I knew was at the end of her rope with the endless caretaking of people who were always at home, the isolation, the thinking that it simply could not go on like this much longer, the buzz of background anxiety that it would—I noticed white spots scattered across my wrist bleached out like the T-shirts I slept in during college, thanks to my nightly applications of acne medicine.

Weird. They definitely hadn't been there the day before.

Two weeks later the spots had fused to become a wide cuff of baby-white skin on both sides of my right wrist. Yes, I had the pale skin of my Irish ancestors, but never this ghostly white, the tiny hairs also suddenly without color.

A week after that, I undressed to find a new constellation of white spots splashed across my right clavicle.

Now I was at the dermatologist, being closely examined through a sort of photographer's loupe. As the doctor looked at my back with intense and silent consideration, I wondered what he was seeing where I couldn't. I realized I was holding my breath.

"Have you been under stress?" he asked, from behind me.

"Uh, yes. Yes, I have."

"What sort of stress?"

"Well, a—a lot of things. It's been a lot." I mean, where to begin? I thought it best to keep my litany of woes in check. He was a dermatologist, not a shrink.

The doctor stood up then, came around to my front, and looked me in the eyes. "I meant *stress*," he said. "Not 'Hmm, yes, I guess I'm sort of stressed.' I'm talking *stress*. Like you were in a car accident."

I went white-hot for a moment, seething at his patronizing tone. Did the last two years not count as sufficiently difficult? Was a pandemic too garden-variety for this guy?

"Oh, I see," I said. "No, nothing like that." Silly me.

He furrowed his brow. "Well. *Something* must have happened, because you've got vitiligo."

He let that sink in for a moment, while my brain scrambled for purchase. Vitiligo. The thing that put Michael Jackson on the road to bleaching himself?

"It's an autoimmune disorder," the doctor explained, as if that made things clearer. "Not contagious, and not fatal. But there also isn't any cure. This doesn't usually happen all of a sudden for someone your age, unless there's a clear trigger. Which is why I asked. One would expect there to have been a sudden shock to the system." He paused. "Or, at least, a life history with a high prevalence of stressful events."

A high prevalence of stressful events? Why, yes. The last two years, the last five, the last ten. This dude didn't know the half of it. No one did, except my therapist. (And even then . . . I hated to make her worry.)

"Anyhow. Vitiligo is not dangerous, but it is progressive," the doctor continued. "Without treatment it could advance rapidly. Even if we *do* treat it, there's no guarantee it will work. But whatever you do, try not to worry about it," he added as he closed my folder. "Because stress can make it worse."

Completely unpredictable, probably unfixable, and worrying too much was also bad. After eighteen months of a pandemic, that sounded pretty familiar.

I went home and did what I always do in the face of a new challenge: compile enough research to teach an intro-level college course. One's immune system can become overactivated, for reasons that are mostly poorly understood, and perceive enemies inside the body where none exist. In the case of vitiligo, the body starts to destroy its own melanocytes, seemingly overnight. And a few months after the doctor told me my pandemic problems weren't serious enough, a study concluded that "Covid-induced stress" could indeed be a trigger for susceptible patients.

I took grim satisfaction in this, certain I had been one of them. But it still didn't fully explain things. Everyone in the world had dealt with the pandemic—or at least the lockdowns—and there hadn't been a massive vitiligo outbreak to match. Was it my personal inability to process those challenges that had made my body start attacking itself?

Or had this been a long time coming, black mold showing up after years of ignoring the slow leaks?

Either way, it was a reckoning it seemed I had earned for myself.

Either way, vitiligo was one more thing that was all my fault.

I'd catch myself thinking like this and then be annoyed that I was being so dramatic and vain. No matter how much the vitiligo spread, the only real risk was to my self-esteem. But it was hard not to dwell on what was happening when it was right there, on my dominant hand, whenever I texted or drove or reached out for something. It was unsettling watching it bloom farther up my arm without being able to do anything to control it. If my body had done this to get my attention, it had worked.

I am nothing if not a fully compliant patient. For the next year, I visited the dermatology unit of the hospital three times a week, putting on tinted goggles and a white shirt carefully cut to expose only the bleached-out parts of me on my right side, covering everything else. Then I would step into a sort of tanning booth, wrapping hospital gowns around my ankles to cover any skin that might have been peeking out above my shoes. Just to put an exclamation point on my overall humiliation, I would then put a starched hospital pillowcase over my head.

"Ready," I would say to the nurse through the closed door.

The booth was claustrophobic, the narrow band UVB light so bright I squinted behind my goggles. The heat and the pillowcase made it hard to breathe. I breathed. *This isn't dangerous. It's just deeply bizarre.* I tried to transform it all in my head to a restorative spa treatment, my dead melanocytes and whatever had caused them bathed by a warm blue light that I told myself represented peace, even though the booth smelled faintly but disconcertingly of popcorn.

And after a few months, miniature brown spots began to appear, tiny faint islands in all the white. Then the margins started to creep in, repigmenting from the edges. My husband noticed a few weeks later. Then my kids did too. Even the doctor clucked approvingly at the next follow-up. I was told my vitiligo was unlikely to spread farther. I was mad at myself for having blown things out of proportion. I was proud of the willpower I had summoned to correct my own body's mistake.

Then, a month later, I looked down while washing my hands at the sink and saw new splashes of white on my hand.

The doctor's underreaction made my heart sink. "That's how this goes," he said. "It gets better one place; then it gets worse somewhere else." He said this as if he had explained it that way before I microwaved myself for a year. He had not, but I should have known; vitiligo is just like everything else, just like life, it turns out. No matter how hard you try, there will be new problems you could not have predicted, old problems you'll never be able to perfectly fix.

Recent research has suggested that sudden-onset vitiligo can occur due to the lingering effects of the coronavirus itself, and not just due to unmanaged stress. In other words, I probably didn't get vitiligo because I overthink things; it happened because I had the bad fortune of catching an early variant of Covid, well before vaccines were available. I prefer this theory, although even then it presumes something in me offering latent possibility, waiting all along for the right moment to burst into existence.

At least I don't have to go to the booth at the hospital three times a week anymore. I've graduated to an at-home unit, a handheld version of those space heaters they outlawed for starting too many fires. I hold it to my wrist before bed three times a week, adding ten seconds each time I use it.

After I built up to four minutes, then six, the unit started getting hot to the touch. *This can't be good,* I thought. *There's no way I should be frying myself for this long.* But when I asked the doctor, he said that wasn't true. "As long as you can handle it, you keep going," he said. "Keep increasing the time."

"Forever?" I asked.

"No, no," he said. "You should stop when you wake up the next morning and you're burned. That's when you'll know that it was too much."

I can stop once the damage is visible.

―――

When I was a girl I was told that I must always raise my hand. Now that same hand is marked, perhaps, by the costs of having raised it too often. I know this about myself: you can count on me to give something my very best shot, even when it's clear that it may never work. Clear to others, that is.

But how will I know to stop sooner next time? It can't be right that I have to wait until I wake up burned. There's something I'm still missing. There's something I still can't quite see.

My vitiligo is with me even in my dreams, although it's different there. In one dream I step out of the shower and look into a mirror, only to find another mirror behind me, so I can see my naked reflection from all sides. From behind, I am entirely patterned with white. My back, the backs of my legs, all of me lacy and beautiful. The patterns are like mandalas, intricate and detailed, parts of me that I—and only I—haven't known were there. How long have I been fooling myself that I have kept things in check, when all along my beautiful damage has been visible to everyone but me?

In my dream, I am not embarrassed that I look this way. I am embarrassed that I had ever thought I could keep these things hidden. I want to see the patterns on my back like my doctor did, up close under his loupe. I yearn to understand how all the dots connect.

I want to reveal every part of myself and heal it with bright light.

You Were Made for This

On the day Jimmy Carter was elected president, I became the oldest of three. There's a picture of seven-year-old me, sitting in our living room's "good chair" holding my infant brother and his still-spongy head, my face showing a dignified understanding of my new role.

I had previously enjoyed bossing around my other, extremely amenable, younger brother, sixteen months my junior. He was always happy to let me decide which Fisher-Price Little People character he would play when we set up all our playsets at once—the parking garage, the schoolhouse, the castle, the airport—to play a multiday game I invented called "Town Carnival." Town Carnival was a world of imagination containing infinite possibility. As our main characters, I would usually assign my brother the little plastic boy with a baseball cap and freckles, a character we named "Butch." We conceptualized Butch as a typical young scamp, adorable and mischievous. I, naturally, would play the smiling, buxom mom with eyelashes for days. Her name was "Mom," and she always knew what was supposed to happen next, but she was also always in a good mood, so Butch was fine with that.

But now our real-life baby brother was going to change things; it could not be otherwise. If two people make a relationship, three make a community, their roles and responsibilities defined in relation to a group. Becoming the firstborn of three meant becoming not just an older sister, but the *oldest* sister. I knew my responsibilities were going to step up, but I accepted them as mine and believed I was up to the challenge. My brother's birth was a coronation of my own, one my second-grade self treated with great solemnity. And while I didn't know it at the time, I would gain three more younger siblings in the years to come.

One cannot measure the depth of experience of an oldest sister simply by the number of younger siblings she has; it's not like being the oldest of six siblings builds exactly twice as much character as being the oldest of three. But it's definitely something. Ten violins playing at once are not ten times louder than one violin—the difference is only a few decibels—and yet, as a whole, they create a sound most of us would agree sure feels bigger.

And while one cannot be more oldest than "oldest," since it's already a superlative, there has to be something that additionally accrues to the oldest daughter of an oldest daughter. In my mother's childhood home, there were a whole lot of violins: she herself was the oldest of eight. When I visited my grandmother's house as a child, I would also see my two aunts who were still in high school, double goddesses with Marcia Brady–straight hair, and my uncle who attended my same grade school, since he was just four years older than I was. I was the oldest of twenty-five grandchildren in that family; my youngest cousin is only three years older than my firstborn. In big families like ours, the generations get so wide they blend right into the ones that follow.

In our house, my two younger sisters would be born while I was in middle school. My youngest brother was not born until I was a sophomore in college, a gap so wide it meant I never lived at home with him for more than a week or two at a time. For years my baby brother would be my "fun fact" for any icebreaker, his very existence—and the fact that both of our parents were the same, although I was almost two decades older—his very existence something remarkable. I adored my youngest brother, and that I was old enough to be his mother further cemented the way I saw myself: as someone whose life circumstances truly set me apart. I was an oldest sister sun, moon, and rising.

My two little sisters were also frequent conversation fodder, since they were "Irish twins" born six days less than a year apart. Their arrivals, while I was in the sixth and seventh grades, proved more than a little embarrassing at recess. ("Don't your parents have a television?" the nastiest boy in school sneered.) But my little sisters also got plenty of positive attention from my peers at dance recitals and Class Day events, and I loved showing them off, two little copies of me in matching monogrammed sweaters. My pride in them was how I imagined a mother's love would feel once I inevitably had children of my own.

There was always something to be done in our house, always someone to be hefted into a highchair and fed a jar of Gerber's, always someone whose coat needed buttoning because they didn't yet know how. But the busy hum was never boring, and a lot of it was sort of fun. I imagine I was a lot less helpful than I thought I was at the time—I spent typically teenaged amounts of time hiding in my room—but I happily read to my siblings, picked up their toys, and "kept an eye on them" whenever my mother was out of the room.

It was shortly after my second sister was born, making me the eldest of five, that my mother gave me a poem she had clipped and saved from a magazine: "The Oldest Sister" by Lois Duncan.

> The oldest sister is born to care.
> Her fingers are fashioned for rolling hair
> And loosing zippers and tying shoes.
> She dwells in a world that she did not choose,
> A world of giggles and shrill demands
> And sticky kisses and clinging hands,
> Where you're not paid when you babysit.
> Yes, oldest sisters all gripe a bit,
> But they love, and they laugh, and they get things done,
> And lucky's the man who can marry one.

"It made me think of you," my mother said. I was delighted by the poem's dead-on sentiments. Not the "rolling hair" part so much, but the rest of it—gosh, yes! Weren't my little sisters constantly in my room touching my stuff while I was at school? Shouldn't I have made a thousand dollars babysitting by now? It was all so true!

But had I griped about it? I wasn't sure I had. I hadn't presented my parents with an invoice for services rendered, hadn't slammed the door. Hadn't yelled that I was sick and tired of helping and didn't want to do it anymore. I was the oldest sister. It was all just what oldest sisters did.

Still, by giving me this poem, my mother was acknowledging that she saw all my contributions. Now I knew that she knew, and it was all the thanks I needed. After all, it was on-the-job experience for the helpmeet I'd become someday. As the poem said, my husband would be so fortunate to have me.

I didn't wonder, at the time, why the "lucky" person in the poem's imagined marriage was the man.

I didn't notice that "griping" was what a person with power calls a complaint they have no obligation to consider.

I didn't ask why being an oldest sister meant living a foregone conclusion. There was work to be done. It fell to me to do my fair share of it. It was enough for me to have that work recognized. Like Lois Duncan (herself an oldest sister), like my mother, I was born to care. And I was good at it. That made me happy.

The Fisher-Price Little People my brother and I played with were beyond basic. They didn't talk or light up; their two-inch-high bodies didn't have arms or legs; their fixed facial expressions offered just the faintest outline of a character. But when my brother and I set up our Town Carnival, each had a fully realized personality and fleshed-out backstory in our minds, and once those stories were defined, they were incredibly fixed. Our Little People didn't grow or change or surprise one another. They were who they had always been, who they always would be. Dad was always riding away to work in his plastic car; Butch was always hatching some harebrained scheme; and Mom was always there, in the Camper or the Happy Houseboat or the Play Family A-Frame House, her merry eyes crinkled above her painted-on smile, living in a world that she did not choose.

Know Your Value

In the spring of my senior year of college I overheard an acting classmate request to borrow someone's car. She needed to drive to New Jersey for a job interview at a regional theater. My ears perked up, and I asked if I might tag along. Acting wasn't a career goal that offered many job interviews; I hoped there would be plenty of auditions, but those were different, with a high rejection rate baked right in. I had observed with slightly increasing distress that my fellow seniors with clearer career paths were acing their LSATs and signing contracts with investment banks. Choosing English and Theater Studies as my majors had seemed obvious for my imagined future as a performing artist, but as the precipice of adulthood neared, it seemed like I had fewer options.

Some of my Theater Studies peers had parents gifting them a year's rent in Manhattan as a graduation present. This was another option definitively unavailable to me. As the oldest of six, it went without saying that I would be on my own financially the day that I graduated. Although I had squandered many of the career connections Yale University might have offered me by setting my heart on, of all things, show business, I was determined to fend for myself. I would show my parents that they were done raising me, that I was good from here on out.

I'd never heard of this regional theater before road-tripping there with my classmate, but the mainstage space was top notch, and the posters in the lobby seemed impressive. We met with the director of educational programs, who explained she was looking for young actors for positions in their touring theater company. After we performed our monologues and endured a few minutes of small talk, she offered both of us yearlong positions right there on the spot, performing Shakespeare and other classic texts for young audiences across the state.

My friend—who was having second thoughts about a job offer that easy to get—said she'd have to think about it. But I immediately said yes. I'd be able to tell my parents that I'd be supporting myself right out of college—and as an actor, no less!

A few months later, on a sweltering August day, I moved my milk-crate night tables to my new home: an apartment above a thumping bar in suburban New Jersey.

This yearlong acting job turned out to be more of an "internship," which included driving the van, stage-managing our company of five, performing, and lugging set pieces in and out of a different New Jersey school every weekday, all for the sub-minimum wage of one hundred dollars per week. The wage was more of a stipend, as our troupe was frequently reminded. We weren't getting health insurance or sick days, and the five of us were expected to pay rent on our shared apartment, in a building that would be condemned two years after we moved out. But we *were* each getting a point a week toward our Actors' Equity union cards! And fifty of those points were all we'd need to become real, card-carrying professionals!

Getting an Actors' Equity card didn't guarantee work either—on the contrary, it meant I would have to start paying union dues while remaining mostly unemployed. But it would be another step toward my becoming a Real Actor. I'd have proof of it right there in my wallet. I would no longer need to say I "wanted to be" an actor when I grew up. I would already be one.

That horizon of legitimacy kept us interns going most days as we performed, without microphones and in gymnasiums full of hundreds of children, either "updated" Shakespeare—with dorky rapping replacing the iambic pentameter—or a didactic play about friendship set against the backdrop of the bombing of Hiroshima. I played Juliet's mother and a Japanese child, respectively, when I wasn't running sound backstage off a giant reel-to-reel deck. Meanwhile, the theater that employed us kept its budgets in the black, thanks to our traveling program's profitability, making nifty use of school systems' allotted budgets for cultural education while paying the five of us so little that my mother's friend suggested I apply for food stamps. I was too proud to consider it, although I was certainly eligible.

At night we interns would heat up soup and grumble about the unfairness of it all. At five a.m. the next morning, we'd get back in the van to do it all again. I was a working actor, which meant I was already beating the odds. My performance as Lady Capulet had moments of real poignancy. I was willing to meet all of it more than halfway.

The same can be said for my relationship at that time, a long-distance thing with my boyfriend Lucas. He was still at Yale, but since I liked campus life far better than I liked my walkup above the dive bar, I was quite happy to spend every other weekend commuting to see him. That was more than enough for me, but not for Lucas, who suggested by mid-October that we allow for the possibility of our seeing other people. It wasn't me, he said. I was terrific. *We* were terrific. It was just that you got to be in college only once. I had to admit he had a point.

After that, our relationship became a don't-ask-don't-tell détente where one of us played the field with great abandon and the other mostly hung out in New Jersey and made mix CDs of songs with significantly relevant lyrics. I told myself a future relationship with Lucas was worth my little bit of near-term heartbreak. We'd laugh about all this someday, the way my siblings and I would laugh when my mother told us how my dad had asked someone else to the Turkey Trot dance their junior year of high school. Things were still great between Lucas and me, at least when we were together. In just a couple more years, we could be together all the time. Until then, I could get by on less, even on days when I'd been openly mocked and laughed at by hundreds of middle-schoolers before ten a.m.

There was one other part of the acting internship that kept me going: we understudied the real, professional actors in the theater's mainstage shows. We all happily learned entire roles, the lines plus all the stage blocking, despite knowing it was extremely unlikely we'd ever go on—because we were assigned roles without much consideration of our suitability to play them.

This was how I, at twenty-two, had become the understudy for the lead in a new play about the later years of suffragist Susan B. Anthony, who had lived well into her eighties. And Bianca, the actress actually playing the role, was a Broadway actress with considerable bona fides. There was some hope that the play might transfer to New York, if this production were successful. Being her understudy meant I could be Real Actress–adjacent. Just by observing, I'd learn so much.

Bianca kept people waiting. She took up space. She hung out during rehearsals in an old-fashioned fur hat, the sort of thing Joan Crawford might have worn to be photographed on the tarmac.

As the pressure on the playwright mounted during run-throughs, and rewrites became extensive, I was summoned to Bianca's dressing room to review the new scenes with her. This was not an opportunity I intended to squander. And Bianca liked me right away—I was polite, I was punctual, and I had a better recall for the monologue that opened Act Two than she did. Bianca began summoning me to run lines before every performance, which I was happy to do; I had nothing much going on back at the interns' apartment, and Lucas was busy with school. (Or, as I tried not to give excessive consideration, busy with someone else.)

Being in Bianca's presence was the opposite of boring. She had a constant and irresistible insistence that things align with her own preferences, something I snickered at until I realized how often it worked. She'd breezily request a particular line reading from another actor so that she might get the laugh instead. She'd interrupt the director's notes to ask if anyone might bring her some very hot tea with extra lemon, and then someone would. "You just put a white light around your intention, darling," she explained, although it seemed simpler than that to me: she was just willing to state what she wanted, while also managing to work in that she was "an actress from the Broadway stage," in a faux-demure tone that suggested the person being asked knew that already. Or should.

I had never met anyone like her.

Opening night finally arrived, and although the play had already had a dozen preview performances, the reviews would finally be published the next morning, the possibility of an off-Broadway transfer dependent on their verdicts. Twenty minutes to curtain, Bianca had her feet up on the shelf in front of the makeup mirror, slurping from a quart of Zabar's matzo ball soup she'd asked the stage manager to heat up for her (not his job).

"Write something for me, won't you?" she purred. "I need to drink this for my vocal cords." She dictated her opening-night thank-you cards to the rest of the cast, then admired my handwriting.

The next morning *The New York Times* review said the play, despite Bianca's "virtuosic" performance, was "forced and far-fetched." It would not get an invitation to transfer. But I did. The same day the play closed, I took the train to Bianca's apartment overlooking Central Park to begin supplementing my meager intern's income as her personal assistant.

A person lacking the ability to set healthy boundaries probably should not accept work as a personal assistant. On the other hand, no one with healthy boundaries would take such a job in the first place. I was a gal Friday who took to Bianca's various demands readily, creating performance riders for personal appearances, putting sheafs of old photos into scrapbooks, and passing hors d'oeuvres at her frequent dinner parties. I had been promised the opportunity to meet the Broadway director Jerry Zaks—and I did, if "meeting" someone can be defined as answering the door and taking his coat.

But wasn't I in the same room with honest-to-goodness theater royalty? The indignities of performing "Rock 'n' Roll Shakespeare!" and shouting above the hoots of fourth graders who couldn't believe what morons we were had worn me down. I couldn't wait to move to Manhattan and work for Bianca all the time—while pursuing my own career, of course. Being in Bianca's orbit was in itself a huge step forward. I was meeting renowned theater professionals, even if I was just telling them where the powder room was. I would work hard, pay my dues, and go to as many open calls as it took. I never doubted that if I kept showing up, someday someone would notice how much more I had to offer.

The struggle part of an actor's life has no expiration date, even for the very successful. Before working for Bianca, I had imagined acting as a before-and-after binary. I figured that once an actor had made it—say, by playing a lead role on Broadway—that actor would be swept away to Permanent Working Actor Oz, where the hardest question faced would be which of their many offers to accept next. But despite Bianca's rocket-ship success, her name on the marquee at the age of just twenty-six—or twenty-two, as she preferred to tell it—I saw firsthand her ongoing fight even to get in the audition room for certain directors and producers.

Bianca's success had come thanks to a certain singularity of purpose that resulted in her having a reputation of Being a Lot. Being Difficult. Which weren't the same thing. Bianca was certainly demanding, but she was also extremely talented, and I'd never seen her throw an actual tantrum. But the reputation had stuck. One day I took a phone call from her long-suffering agent reporting that she would not be getting an audition for Neil Simon's new play after all, because Simon had personally and flatly refused to see her. I was crushed on Bianca's behalf. If monomaniacal drive was what it took for a woman to break through in show business, was it fair to malign her for that quality once she was a star? I determined that I would never be seen as a diva, no matter what successes I might have, since that label came with considerable costs.

But would success even be possible without a willingness to be pushy?

The trick, I decided, was to be driven without ever being perceived as such. To work tirelessly to get ahead while making sure everyone still liked me.

Bianca, at least, couldn't get enough of me. "Can you come again tomorrow?" became "See you at the dot of eight, darling. We really must start on time." Soon I was spending more waking hours in her apartment than I was in my own. My days at Bianca's became an endless fount of funny stories for my friends and my roommate Michael, another aspiring actor. Bianca would start dictating a letter, then interrupt it to start a different one. She would scribble addresses and phone numbers on torn bits of napkins and envelopes, then have me turn her apartment upside down to find them. Her cyclonic disorganization meant she simply couldn't survive without me, and so for the next three years I accompanied her basically everywhere, hanging out on her soap opera sets and at her voice lessons, holding her various tote bags and taking on the secondary anxiety of how late she was for whatever she was supposed to be doing next.

My own career was by now my second shift, this one mostly on nights and weekends, doing sketch comedy in bars and nearly incomprehensible experimental theater in various basements across the Lower East Side. It was hard to know if I was really getting anywhere appearing in plays where those on stage often outnumbered the paying audience members, but I was determined to keep showing up. The trickier part was making room for my own dreams in a life as chaotic as Bianca's.

"I need you tomorrow at seven-thirty sharp," she said one afternoon. "I'll run the reservoir, and then we'll start on my lines for the audition at eight-fifteen."

"I—actually can't come that early," I said. "I have an audition tomorrow morning also."

"What for?"

"It's a dance call. For *Grease*." (The bus-and-truck national tour. I'd have to get in the open-call line before seven a.m. with headshot and character shoes, but my roommate knew the assistant director's assistant, and he said he'd get me in.)

"Darling, I have a *callback*. For a *series*. Everyone knows those open calls don't mean anything."

This was true. No one got cast from open calls. Except my college classmate who had just snagged a leading Broadway role from an open call, and who would perform on national television at the Tony Awards later that spring. But I mean, exactly! My classmate's incredible luck was the exception that only proved stuff like that never really happened. Bianca was right: her auditions were more important. My own could wait. Heaven knew

Bianca couldn't manage a callback without me; she needed me to run lines with her while she found her shoes, rang for the elevator, and yelled instructions to her housekeeper.

One summer day she felt so underprepared she had me jump in the back seat of the cab with her so she could practice her audition scene a few more times during the twenty-five-minute ride downtown.

"I can't read the scenes. I'm sorry," I said. I have always had trouble reading in the car; in the back seat of a jerky taxi, it was a definite no-go.

"Why not?" she asked.

"I get really car sick. I'll throw up."

"Oh. Well. That's all right, darling," Bianca said, nodding reasonably. "We'll just run the lines until you feel like you're *about* to throw up. Then you can stop."

So I did. This was what willingness to pay one's dues looked like. Would I take notes for Bianca's new one-woman show while she prepared for a luncheon, bathroom door open, completely naked? Of course. Would I go back over to her apartment on the way home from a sketch comedy performance because she couldn't find a phone number? No problem. Would I answer an early-morning call from a sobbing fifth grader (Bianca's child) who couldn't get the printer to work, get said printer to work, then deliver the history paper to the school principal's office with a note for the teacher explaining that it was all my fault? Yes, yes, and yes.

I was complaining to Lucas about all this on the phone one night, my usual litany of *Wait till you hear what Bianca did now*, when he interrupted me with an uncharacteristic flash of frustration.

"Quit," he said.

"What?"

"I've been hearing you talk about Bianca for two and a half years. Quit. Or else I don't want to hear you talk about it anymore. Those are your choices."

I'd never heard Lucas express a boundary like this before. I wasn't sure I'd heard *anyone* express a boundary like that before. But he was right, so I made the only possible choice: I didn't talk about Bianca to him anymore.

The other option, quitting, was obviously unthinkable. Bianca needed me too much. Avoiding the topic would be far easier, since the list of things Lucas and I didn't talk about, a few years into our long-distance and nonmonogamous relationship, was already pretty long.

But very soon the difficult parts of my relationship with Lucas, which to me all seemed to be the result of our being apart, would disappear. Just a couple months of separation were left before Lucas would move to New York City; all that was left was his summer acting internship in the Berkshires. It was the same sort of first step I'd taken in my own career, except this wasn't "Rock 'n' Roll Shakespeare!" Lucas had gotten a walk-on role in a mainstage show. My bags were packed to go see him perform.

He called me the night before. "Don't come," he said.

I felt like I was falling.

"Why?" I asked, catching myself, willing my voice to remain calm.

"It will be weird."

"Why?" I asked again, knowing why, of course, but wanting him to say it. He was seeing someone else. But that wasn't a problem! I had agreed to accept such things. For just a little while longer, I still would.

"I don't think you should come, because, well, I'm in a relationship," Lucas said. "And it would be really uncomfortable for her if you showed up."

I hung up, unpacked my bag, avoided my roommate Michael's pointed questions, and stayed in the city that hot July weekend. Not only was Lucas in a relationship, it seemed that it was not with me.

But we hadn't actually broken up. Had we? And wasn't he allowed to have one final summer fling? If I simply didn't tell anyone else what he had said, then there was no need to engage with what it all really meant. Yes, my "boyfriend" was considering someone else's feelings far above my own, but couldn't I choose to see that as a test of my own ability to love?

I knew how to do this. I knew how to wait. I knew how to pay my dues. I had been given two choices, and I would not quit. But I would, per Lucas's preference, stop talking about it.

I did try to quit working for Bianca. Several times. She wouldn't let me. At least that was what I told myself as her demands increased and my resentment grew. She became short-tempered. I yelled back. My own career was becoming improbably and suddenly larger: my sketch comedy group had signed with a big agency. Then we got a development deal with NBC. We would have six months to write a season's worth of sketches that we'd shoot in the *Saturday Night Live* studios during their summer hiatus. We would each be paid six figures, and our offices would become available on the first of the month.

My first reaction was elation. My second reaction was dread at the idea of telling Bianca I could not be her assistant anymore.

She reacted much more calmly than I had feared. "Well, this is very good, darling," she said. "These development deals never go anywhere, but this is still a big step for you. Did I have anything to do with this, by the way? Did you get to William Morris through me?"

"Uh, no," I said. The coat-taking at her dinner parties had not really paid off in terms of making connections.

"Well, I certainly wish you all the best, sweetheart." She took my hands, squeezed them. "Of course, you'll train your replacement before you go."

I was allowed to leave, just as soon as I found another me.

This proved to be a Rumpelstiltskin-level challenge, a task with a built-in guarantee of failure. After two weeks of "training," my first replacement quit. Two weeks after that, the second replacement stopped showing up. I, who somehow was still the one working for Bianca, tried putting a white light around my intention. "I have to stop working here now," I explained. "I have an office at Rockefeller Center! And I'm supposed to be there right now. We have to write an entire television show in the next two months!"

"Of course, yes, I totally understand," Bianca replied. "In that case, why don't we just move our work sessions to Sunday mornings?"

Bianca's inability to hear what I was telling her was impressive, I thought, on the walk to her apartment the following Sunday morning—although her powers of denial were also in play, and those may have been more contagious. Lucas had continued writing letters to me all summer, ones in which he mostly professed his great romantic confusion of loving two people at once. But since I was pretty sure I was one of those people, I chose to see this as the final test. His summer-stock spell would be broken as soon as he moved to New York City. All I had to do was wait it out.

I maintained the willing suspension of disbelief of an eleven-year-old on Christmas Eve until summer ended, and Lucas finally moved to New York. He gave me the number of the friend's apartment where he'd be crashing for a few days. When I called that number, a woman answered the phone.

"He's—um—not available right now," she said. It was clear from the sound of her voice this was a lie. "Would you like to leave a message?"

I would not. But Lucas's message to me had finally been received.

My roommate Michael ran a similar sort of telephone interference for me at our apartment that autumn, screening all calls whenever he was home. If it was Lucas or Bianca, I was not free at the moment, even if I was standing right there. If Michael went out, he'd listen to the messages on our answering machine when he got back, deleting the ones we both knew I didn't need to hear.

The "Ames, call me. *As soon as possible.* Where is the videotape of my guest appearance on *Law and Order*?"

The "Hey. It's me. Hey there. I'm just . . . I'm thinking of you. Give me a call."

Michael would always give me the gist of the messages he had erased, but we agreed my not listening to them was the best way to ensure that I did not respond.

Those answering machine invitations would keep coming sporadically for a long time. So long that I would meet someone, fall in love. Start living with him instead of with my roommate, Michael.

So long that I would write that TV show.

So long that I would finally use that Actors' Equity card.

So long that I would get a cell phone and start listening to my own messages.

One was from Bianca. "Come over for coffee," she said. "Call me, sweetheart. I miss you."

I missed Bianca too. It had been years. So much had changed for me. Now I had someone who loved me back. Now I was the one making Neil Simon's callback list. There was so much for me to share with her.

A few days later I waited for Bianca at the same dining room table where we used to work together. Ten minutes after I arrived, she came barreling out of her bedroom, buttoning her blouse with one hand, fumbling in her purse for her lipstick with the other, calling to her housekeeper. "Daniela, where is my script? I left it right here on this table last night!" she yelled. "I'm terribly late!"

I joined the search and found the script between the couch cushions. Would I mind quickly running the lines with Bianca? I did not mind. Would I join her in the elevator, since she was running late, and she was so sorry she didn't have time for coffee after all? Sure, no problem. Would I just jump in the back of the taxi for the ride to Midtown so she could run the scenes just once or twice more?

No. I did not get in the car.

As I walked back to the subway, I was mostly mad at myself, for biding my time until the day I would be seen. For not having known when to stop trying.

Bianca taught me that if I was too demanding, people would not like me.

But demanding nothing meant people would never see me at all.

Do What Matters

As a child, I went to Sunday Mass every week. I really never complained about it, although I wasn't much of a rebel to begin with. Weekly Mass attendance was so deeply ingrained an expectation in my family, my school, and my neighborhood that it never occurred to me to wonder whether I wanted to go.

I liked some parts of Mass very much: my grandfather's tenor ringing loud and clear in the choir, the way they'd turn off all the lights on Christmas Eve so we could sing "Silent Night" to a candlelit baby Jesus in the manger, and the missalettes that enabled me to follow along with the readings each week. The Sunday readings for Catholic Mass work their way through a three-year cycle, during which the four Gospels telling the life of Jesus are covered pretty much in full. Then it starts all over again. For me, this meant reencountering these stories afresh at each stage of my own development, and while most of them were interesting enough, there was one reading that frustrated me more each time I heard it: the story of Mary and Martha.

As the story goes, Jesus was invited by a woman named Martha to take respite at her home from his journeying and preaching. Soon after, Jesus was seated in Martha's living room blowing the minds of those gathered around him, particularly Martha's sister, Mary, who was lounging at Jesus's feet. Martha—who, as the evangelist Luke tells us, was "burdened with much serving"—comes into the living room, sees Mary sitting there, and asks Jesus to please tell her sister to give her a hand. But Jesus replies, "Martha, you are anxious and worried about many things. There is need of only one thing. Mary has chosen the better part, and it will not be taken from her."

Even as a third grader, this annoyed me to no end. Okay, yes: if a deity in human form comes over to your house, you're probably supposed to drop everything and just hang out. But once it looks like he and his friends are planning on staying for dinner, someone has to prepare that meal. And if not Martha, who?

Then my young mind would get even more stuck. Hadn't it been elsewhere established that Jesus could feed thousands of people with a couple of fish and five loaves of bread? I could only assume that no one had clued Martha in about this, which might have saved her a lot of trouble. Instead, everyone in that room gave Martha the old "There you go again, worrying about stuff that doesn't matter. Also, when will dinner be ready exactly? We're starving."

Every time this reading came around, the priest would try to put a useful spin on it: God doesn't want us to work too hard. God wants us to make time for what matters, i.e., God. But no matter what angle the priest took, I'd still carry home a tiny candle of spite in my heart on Martha's behalf. Martha didn't *want* to work too hard. People who say, "The chores can wait!" are rarely the ones who are going to have to do them. If Mary got to just hang out, someone should, at the very least, have thanked Martha for doing Mary's "worse part" for her.

Do What Matters

People in this world are either Marthas or Marys, and women are certainly socialized to be the Marthas, which always made me as jealous of Mary as I was annoyed. How could Mary just hang out and relax knowing there was work to be done? Even as a third grader, I knew I couldn't be a Mary if I tried.

As a grown-up, I try to tell myself I *could* be a Mary, at some hypothetical future time when I'm not as busy as I am at that moment. Also, I'm always busy.

For me, being productive has always equaled being happy, those two things increasing in direct proportion to each other. "Outer order, inner calm" is how happiness expert Gretchen Rubin puts it. Her advice for a happier life presumes that neater, tidier surroundings will increase anyone's relaxation—and therefore happiness—as will a to-do list with lots of things already crossed out. It's all true for me, which is why I try to live by Gretchen's "one-minute rule," stating that anything that takes less than sixty seconds is best done right then. Don't wait to RSVP to the party, just do it. Put the boots back in their shoebox, the shredded cheese back in the refrigerator. Don't let your to-dos pile up. Who wouldn't be happier doing things this way?

Apparently, every other person I live with. There is no yogurt lid, phone charger, or piece of mail that is not tossed aside to be dealt with at some future point that never seems to arrive. When my husband returns from traveling, the first thing he'll do is unpack his suitcase all over our bedroom, seeding the entire room with a fine layer of vacation dust. Socks on the desk, crumpled receipts on the nightstand. He tells me it just makes him feel better to unpack right away.

"But you're only *kind of* unpacking," I tell him. "This is way worse than if you just left it in the suitcase." Nonetheless, for him, outer I-See-Everything-I-Own-Which-Might-Be-Laundry-Now-But-Maybe-Not somehow equals inner calm, and our bedroom will usually remain that way for several more days, because he's already pretty happy, so the one-minute rule need not apply.

I find more satisfaction in clearing my decks, both literally and metaphorically. If I am surprised by five free minutes, I'm never at a loss as to what to do with them. The strangers who are my seatmates on airplanes usually sit down and get busy choosing a movie; I get busy with a running list on my laptop called STUFF TO DO ON PLANE.

I keep said list nested among many others on an app called Workflowy, advertised as "the productivity app for people who hate productivity apps." Are there any such people? Not among the productive. And I love productivity apps even more than I love being productive, because playing with a new toy that promises to help me get more done feels useful while also deftly serving as a new way to procrastinate. There is no article titled "Seven Tools Guaranteed to Make You More Productive!" that I won't drop everything to read immediately. "Stop Reading Articles Emailed to You by Substack" might be a useful tool to list first, although that particular advice never seems to appear.

If there's a way to get more done out there, I've probably already given it a spin. Besides Workflowy, the apps I have installed on my phone and laptop include Evernote, Slack, Todoist, FollowUpThen, Airtable, and IFTTT (If This, Then That). I also use paper-based productivity systems: the Time-Block Planner, the Intelligent Change Productivity Planner, the Ink+Volt Dashboard Deskpad. The names of these systems promise states of aerodynamic, abundant bliss, increasing your volume of work accomplished while simultaneously decreasing your stress. The Autofocus system promises you will "Get Everything Done." The Getting Things Done system, altogether different, guarantees "stress-free productivity." The Full Focus Planner will set you back forty-nine dollars—and you'll need to buy a new one every three months—but for "the planner that changes lives," how can that be anything but an incredible bargain?

One shortcoming of all these planning systems is that they are, in and of themselves, quite a bit of work. Quarterly goal reviews and pages of reflections on your "big wins" might help you chart a more productive course going forward, but where is one supposed to find the time to complete them?

To quantify where such gaps of free time might exist, there are additional apps that promise to save you, lazy unproductive person, from the sins of your own distractibility. An app called Freedom blocks access on all your devices, so you can't look at Instagram on your phone instead of on your laptop. SelfControl blocks access to designated websites for whatever time frame you desire; once you turn it on, even rebooting your computer won't get you out of Focused Work Jail. I am using SelfControl right now as I write these words. A skull icon lurks on my desktop, beaming threats at me with the black holes of its eyes: *I'm going to kill you if you try to look at Facebook.* It's both saving me from the deadly stickiness of the social media algorithms and warning me of the consequences if I disobey: less accomplishment, more shame.

Sometimes I forget and try to launch a blacklisted site during a blocked moment of creativity, only to remember that, oh, right, I *can't* open LinkedIn, because I turned on software to prevent that from happening, because my frailty is too great, as I have just proven once again.

Here is where the efforts to improve my productivity get complicated: no matter how much I do, I didn't get it *all* done. My list is still there with more things on it, showing me that I might have done more. But making lists, productivity experts agree, is the necessary first step. One must understand the full scope of possible work, of the things one *could* be doing, in order to begin to tame the beast. And if the length of your list consistently outpaces your ability to get through it, it's just a matter of increasing your efficiency. Of setting timers, breaking down the goals, batching your responses, eating the frog first.

Still, even when I do all these things, when I plan what phone call I'm going to return while I walk the dog, what article I'm going to read on the subway, what chapter I'm going to edit while I get my hair colored, my list seems to spool further and further away from me. Then I think, *I just have to try a little harder. I just have to go a little faster. I can relax later. Once I'm finished*.

And yet, despite trying every productivity system—and sometimes several at once—I was never reaching the "more time to enjoy long walks and go on that vacation!" finish line promised by these methods and systems. The harder I worked, the more I engaged with my own overwhelm. What was I doing wrong?

I began looking for answers, as one does, on YouTube, watching interviews with the founders of all these methods. Amid their respective supersonic outputs, they all seemed to have at least enough time left over to interview one another. I watched a few of these interviews before the obviousness of what separated me from these paragons of productivity hit me: all of them,

Do What Matters

without exception, were men. And if they were parents or caregivers, it wasn't a topic that merited mention. These men were people with the power to decide what they wanted to do next, then the freedom to do that thing without unwanted intrusion. These men didn't need Virginia Woolf to tell them they needed rooms of their own; they all had them already. And who would dare interrupt the founder of the Turbo Quantum Achievement System to ask him where the Nutella was?

You can create a productivity groove in which you ignore your emails from HR until noon each day and disable your itchy Instagram finger, but you can't ignore the dog walking into the room and throwing up. You can't put your phone on Do Not Disturb mode if your kid has a peanut allergy and the school nurse always calls the default parent, who is you. To "achieve more while doing less," as the Full Focus Planner promises, one must first have the luxury of ever being able to do one thing at a time. For women with too much to do, monotasking usually requires establishing a replacement village first, then pushing aside the nagging feeling that our own priorities are too selfish to fully embrace.

And even if you do manage to put on the noise-canceling headphones and shut the door, your loved ones' ideas of what qualifies as a worthy interruption may vary from your own. When my youngest child was about four years old, she once flung the shower door wide while I was mid-shampoo to ask me, with some urgency, which was farther from New York City: California or "the whole wide world."

For women with too much to do, the things that impede our productivity are not caused simply by laziness or procrastination. For women with too much to do, the almost-overdue permission list for the field trip must go atop the list of important things to do next—unless we follow the one-minute rule and just dash that permission slip off right then, following that one-minute rule again, and again, for the rest of our lives.

There will always be something I could do quickly, right now, and cross it off my list, and while knowing that makes me more productive, it also creates an unrest that is hard to call happiness. It also makes me kind of a Martha as a partner and a parent. I watch my teenagers scrolling through their phones ten, twenty, thirty minutes after waking, and I want to say, "Don't you have a paper due Monday? Don't you have practice in an hour? Did you write back to Mr. Hannan about that thing?" Half the time I say it and absorb their irritation; half the time I don't say it and absorb my own anxiety at their tasks left unaccomplished. *Why can't you just send that email already?* I want to scream. *We've been talking about it for a week! Your phone is* in *your hand! Have you never heard of the one-minute rule?* But I've learned that my saying any of those things will not only increase their irritation, but also, paradoxically, reduce their productivity, thanks to their sense that ignoring what one's mother says is always the more honorable choice. Such things therefore stay on my own mental list, saved for that elusive moment when the other person might be more receptive. When reforwarding the insurance guy's deductible question to my spouse, I've learned to put RESPONSE REQUIRED in the subject line. That almost always works, but the ten percent chance it won't means I have to move "get back to insurance guy" from my main list to another, secondary list: Waiting to Hear Back.

The inevitable result is the "invisible workload" that society seems to finally be acknowledging, although we may still underestimate just how taxing it can be. Sociologist Allison Daminger calls it "cognitive labor" and explains that any task a caregiver completes has four steps: anticipating the need, identifying options for meeting the need, making the decision, and, finally, monitoring the progress. Using this math, each "invisible" thing on the list of a woman with too much to do is actually four things. No wonder we can't seem to shorten our lists. No wonder I'm finding the methods that tell me I should "do less in order to do more" somewhat lacking. That sort of overhead is beyond my ability to ever complete, no matter how much I get done before eight a.m.

Which isn't to say that I'll stop trying, or that attempting greater productivity is always useless. I wrote this book one page at a time by getting up before the rest of my family and hiding from all the "this will take only a minute" demands I usually find impossible to ignore. Finding the time to do something this important to me *is* possible, but only if I make myself invisible while I do it. Only if I take the time that is required away from time I would otherwise be sleeping or exercising or connecting with friends. If I need to find more overhead, my basic needs are where I will trim the fat.

⁓

Productivity-chasers feel like better people when we accomplish more. We attach moral meaning to "inbox zero." And of course there is an exhilaration that accompanies the checking off of every single thing everyone has asked of us that day. But anything short of completion is not quite enough. And even when we manage to achieve a blank-screen nirvana, fifty new emails will ruin it all by the next morning. The world will always make more work for us to do. No nesting categories of worthiness, no color-coded triage systems will stop it from coming. We are all Lucy Ricardo in the candy factory, and keeping up with our workloads just means the pace of production will be increased until something breaks. Or until the people who run the factory consider whether there might be another way of doing things.

In the 1960s an engineer named Taiichi Ohno developed a system for Toyota's manufacturing plant in Japan to make the inefficiencies in that automaker's processes more visible. In Ohno's framework, called Kanban, tasks to be completed became cards that moved through visible, logical steps toward completion, allowing companies like Toyota to streamline their systems and quickly find the bottlenecks.

Forty years later, another engineer named Jim Benson adapted Kanban for personal use. I was first introduced to the idea of Personal Kanban in Oliver Burkeman's book *Four Thousand Weeks*, and since the method required two of my favorite things—Sharpies and Post-it notes—I knew I had to give it a whirl.

The first step of Personal Kanban entails writing each task on a Post-it note, then placing all those notes in a column labeled *Ready*.

Then you pick three Post-it notes—just three—and move them to a column called *Doing*.

Then you do those three things. As each task is completed, you move its Post-it note to a third column: *Done*.

Here's the rub: Personal Kanban requires limiting your work in progress. You can't have more than three cards in the Doing column at once. You can't add anything to the Doing column until you've made room for it by moving another task card to

Done. Personal Kanban requires limiting your works in progress.

In most things I am a rule follower, but my Doing column currently lists no less than ten time-sensitive items, including booking my son's oral surgery, arranging parking at the airport for next week, and finding the error hiding somewhere on a Q3 spreadsheet. The only thing on that list that's just for me? Scheduling my second shingles vaccine. The only thing more unappealing than moving that task to the Done column is, I suppose, adding "recovering from shingles" to Doing.

Still, making my work visible has had an improbably calming effect. After creating my first round of physical Post-it notes, seventy-two tasks in the "Ready" column, my inability to complete them all was right there in front of me, not my imagination and impossible to escape. As it turns out, my spouse's form of unpacking—spreading everything out all over our bedroom, then leaving it there for three or four days—wasn't so cuckoo. He observes the scope of his undone task for a little while, knowing he'll get to it eventually. It's not like he'll forget; how can he, when it's all laid out in front of him?

When I started making my Ready list tangible and visible, something I could touch and move, I was finally able to see all that I had to do. It was not only quite large; it was, simply, too much. Jim Benson says this is the entire point of Personal Kanban. "We cannot do more than we are capable of doing," he writes. "This should seem obvious, but it's not." My list isn't too long because I procrastinate. My list is too long because there are too many things on it. Understanding the impossibility of the thing I used to beat myself up about has led to more moments of inner calm than any attempt I've made to work better or faster.

I *am* productive. I do a lot. I'll just never do it all. Which means I can give myself some slack.

I'd always considered slack the opposite of productivity. Slack was not pulling with all your strength. Slack was doing nothing even when there was work to be done. Slack was Mary hanging out in the living room while Martha made dinner.

But in Kanban, slack is the open space that lets a workflow adjust, either to unexpected additional demands or to a day when something that usually takes ten minutes takes ninety instead. Without any open space at all, you run the risk of gridlock. One hiccup and you'll remain frozen right where you are, getting nothing done at all. And that's usually when someone will tell you that you really need to lighten up.

If some slack should always exist amid whatever "Doing" I assign myself, I can stop trying to optimize every moment of my day in service of some imaginary future leisure. I can stop thinking that I must finish everything that is Ready before I can rest.

But I can also stop beating myself up for being the sort of deeply unchill person who sees what needs to be done in the first place. Marthas just see those things, and as incomprehensible as it might seem to me, the Marys in the world might not. Or else they figure the Marthas have got it, and why wouldn't they? We always have before. The universe will always be there to make more—and more of it will be handed to the Marthas, since we've proven ourselves so good at crossing things off. Getting better at getting things done just means being given more to do.

It's hard to give myself permission to do something that *I* need next, even when my colleague is still expecting that press release before end of business day, even when my daughter just yelled down the hall that she can't find her shoes. But finding peace in chaos doesn't mean ordering the chaos first. It means just stopping. Wanting to relax is enough of a reason, even when there is more to be done.

I'd prefer outer order to create my inner calm, but I'm working on getting a little closer to outer catastrophe, inner calm. Outer "just circling back on that project we discussed," inner calm. Outer "just wondering if you've thought about what's for dinner," inner calm. Outer "Mom, my wrist still hurts from last week," inner calm. I don't have to fix all those things right now. Maybe just some of them. Maybe just one more email before bed. Maybe just one more Kanban card moved to Done for today.

I can accept that I can't do it all, then try again.

Do this thing next. Limit my works in progress.

I am a work in progress. I am the better part.

The Truth Will Set You Free

I kept a diary only once in my life: the year I graduated from eighth grade, the year of Sister Benedicta. That December my father gave me a handsome leather-bound journal whose cover had been stamped "E. F. Hutton," which probably means he'd been gifted it at a holiday party. Something about that diary must have spoken to my father, telling him that his adolescent daughter was its more appropriate recipient. He had always thought I could be a writer, was always encouraging me to finish the ghost stories I would start writing on boring afternoons only to never pick them up again. It was a gift that therefore contained an assignment, one I took to with my usual immediate seriousness.

I want to really get in the habit of writing in here, the first entry reads. *It's a good way of relieving pent-up feelings.* Or at least I imagined that to be a diary's purpose, which was why it was so important that a girl my age had one. Like most thirteen-year-old females, I understood myself to be blossoming into the most important moments of a truly exceptional life. My changing body, my new desire to individuate from my parents, my sudden seeing of the world through boy-colored glasses—each day brought events and emotions I'd clearly want to remember in minute detail once I was living the boring life of a grown-up. What better place to memorialize such historic times than a diary, long a rite of passage for adolescent girls with deep thoughts?

> *I can keep this and read it over and over, remembering the good times I had this day. I can never relive this second I am writing this again, but I can remember it.*

Implicit in this statement were two assumptions: that whatever I wrote about was worth remembering, and that I might not remember it at all were it not for this careful record I was creating with a proper sense of its grandeur and import. A teen girl's diary mattered. I had recently raced through *Go Ask Alice* by Anonymous, the "shocking true diary" of a teenage runaway drug addict. The decades since have revealed the true author of this book to be a Mormon youth counselor out to scare kids straight, and not a fifteen-year-old at all, but like most readers at the time I took the diary to be genuine and its heroine's (admittedly completely implausible) trajectory incredibly absorbing. After Alice's drink was spiked at a slumber party, she went from accidental LSD addiction to life on the streets in less than a year. The book's ending shook me up enough that I wrote about it in my own diary:

> *She died. She almost made it, was building her life up again, and she* died. *I am so glad that this girl kept a diary so faithfully. I don't at all. I'm going to try harder.*

The Truth Will Set You Free

The world was a dangerous place for teenage girls, even ones who didn't hang out at Haight-Ashbury. I had to be very careful. I had to try harder. I had to keep precise records in my diary as I went. If I did so, this self-accountability might, over time, lead to my overall improvement.

The other foundational text of this time in my life was *Young Miss* magazine, which came in the mail every month with exciting promises trumpeted across its cover:

SOLVE YOUR BOY PROBS!
GET HIM TO NOTICE YOU!
THESE FASHIONS WILL SOLVE YOUR FIGURE PROBLEMS!
TURN FRIENDSHIP INTO ROMANCE!

Young Miss offered about as many truthful takeaways as *Go Ask Alice* did, but I took its every word as bedrock. My life was one big project, and my project was the curation of myself. There was nothing about me I didn't have to tighten or tauten or fix.

First off, I had a figure problem. Being happy with your own body as it was? Not an option. You could identify as a Skinny Minnie or as a Pleasingly Plump Paula, but you had to pick a side. After a few months' worth of quizzes I deduced that my figure was pear-shaped. I took note of how I might dress to accentuate my assets and conceal my regrettable "bottom-heaviness," an insecurity I would carry with me for decades.

After additionally ascertaining that my face was heart-shaped and my color season was winter, I tried out new signature options on a blank page of my diary. My name needed to *look* like my personality when I wrote it. The Palmer Method version of my penmanship was sorely lacking in individuality. After finding none of my own experiments sufficiently exciting, I sent two dollars and fifty cents of the money I made walking one of my cousins home from school to an address in the *Young Miss* classified ads. I received, a few weeks later, about a dozen new options for how I might sign my name. I decided on one with a capital "A" that looked like a star. I practiced it over and over until it felt second nature, felt like me.

I used that signature throughout my diary on the accountability statements I made for myself, sternly worded for my eyes only:

> *Monday, Feb 7 - I have just ordered "Cashew Crunchies" from the school candy sale. I am hereby promising that I will only eat two a day, allowing myself two indulgences, at which times I can eat three. Every time I'm tempted I will read this promise, go check my weight, and exercise.*

Reader, I did no such thing. I remember eating about six of these rather large chocolate patties each day after school for a week, stopping only when my stomach hurt, then self-condemning until bedtime. Because I had the preposterous metabolism of a teenager, my weight remained wholly unaffected, even though I broke the exercise promise as well. Outside of my diary, I rarely thought about my weight or my physical fitness, except for desultory weekly ballet and jazz classes where the breaks during which my teacher chatted with her elderly mother in the lobby were longer than the parts in which we danced.

So what was happening here? Why the "hereby" and the "indulgences"? I was performing the concern about my weight that seemed an important part of the teenage-girl job. I was imitating the meticulous attention to food that the *Young Miss* models swore by in its pages. A school candy sale was no moment to relax. Cashew Crunchies weren't something a girl could just eat with abandon. Cashew Crunchies led to temptation! A girl could safely consume them only if she had an exhaustive plan.

Once a method for staving off figure problems was in place, it was time to turn to an even more crucial component of my self-improvement project: fostering my friendships with the opposite sex. It was clear I had "boy probs," although it seemed that every reader of *Young Miss* did, because in this case the advice offered was one-size-fits-all. In order to get boys to notice me, I had to adopt a boy-craziness I didn't exactly feel and perform a version of teen femininity that would be maximally appealing.

> *Yesterday was my jackpot day on boys. Dan H. has been bugging Tina to ask me out for him. On top of that, yesterday Dave O. asked me out for Joe. Then Richie F. asked me to dance with him on Awards Night. I said, "Sure, Richie!" Then, today in the hall, he put his arm around my waist! I just turned around and said, "RICHIE!!?!!" He said, "Sorry, Amy," and smiled his goofy smile. The problem is, I don't want to go out with any of these guys!*

Which was fine, because I did not actually "go out with any of these guys," although page after page of my diary recalls the ongoing machinations of who used to like whom but didn't anymore, and whether or not Jimmy Moloney liked me. Facts to consider: he sat next to me on the bus; he waited for me in the hallways; other girls came up to me at lunchtime to say "Jimmy

Moloney likes you." I mean, who could say? It was just so hard to be certain. And how did I feel about Jimmy Moloney?

I think I like him, a little.

Jimmy Moloney lived on my street and rode his bike past my house every afternoon on his paper route. He was good at Wiffle ball and perfectly nice, but when I thought of Jimmy Moloney my primary emotion was relief that he—that any boy at all—might like me, more than any sort of reciprocal feeling. Although Jimmy Moloney's name appears in my diary more than any other boy's, as far as my true romantic yearnings at that age, there was really only one name on the list: Eric Benedetti.

Eric was different—a little quiet, super-cute, twinkly eyes. He never called me "Brainiac"; he didn't tease anyone, not like most of the other boys did. While I was (mortifyingly) quite a bit taller than he was, I could certainly wait until he grew. And even if he remained four-foot-eleven forever, my love could see past that. I had waited since sixth grade for Eric Benedetti to notice me, holding my breath every time he walked by and liking him so much that I couldn't even make eye contact. For the benefit of Jimmy Moloney, however, I practiced the bizarre mating rituals of a large-feathered bird.

My plan with Jimmy M. seems to be working! My approach, at first, was subtle. I would be my enthusiastic self until I saw him or spoke to him. Then I would act very shy. Well, I think it's working. He smiles at me real goofy. So now it's Phase II. He's beginning to act distant to me, so I'll be myself again. I'll keep switching back and forth! That'll be sure to get his attention!

I was willing to expend hours of mental energy on these social pursuits, even if I was the only one to whom they made even potential sense. If any of these schemes did manage to get Jimmy Moloney's attention, it was probably a passing consideration, as he lined up for kickball at recess, whether I had perhaps suffered some sort of head injury. I do not think Jimmy Moloney's inner monologue had much of me in it. Neither did he feel any pressure to establish status with the girls in 8 Blue in order to get ahead in the world. Jimmy Moloney did not have a multiphase plan for attracting my attention. Why would he? He was already getting rather too much of it.

Meanwhile, Eric Benedetti, the boy whom I actually liked, was not only too important to try this performance art on—he was too important to talk about in my diary at all.

In his 1967 paper "Egocentrism in Adolescence," psychologist David Elkind suggested that adolescents—and female adolescents, in particular—believe their emotions and experiences to be completely unique. Elkind called this belief a "personal fable, a story which he or she tells himself and which is not true," and suggested that teenage diaries provide particularly eloquent examples. My own diary offered personal fable on every page, alternating between two different types of lies in order to hold it all up. The first was this fake-it-till-you-make-it performance of a confident, boy-crazy teenage girl. The other untruths I told were lies of omission, crafting my narrative with its ideal reader in mind: a future version of myself, whose success as a grown-up would presumably depend on her having had the correct formative experiences.

HAPPY TO HELP

I've decided to make another promise: only write happy things in here.

I attempted to write into existence a carefree, laughing adjunct to the girls I saw on the covers of *Young Miss*, decreasing the yawning distance between their clearly very exciting lives and my own. The teen models laughed with their girlfriends while wearing berets, linking their arms and literally kicking up their heels with gaiety, or adorably knock-kneeing for the photographer, whose gaze they often acknowledged.

I've always considered myself popular in general, but now I'm moving up. I'm getting more boyfriends, as in friends who are boys!

I did not, in reality, consider myself "popular in general." But *Young Miss* promised I could close that gap with a lot of hard work. I didn't have to become someone else, as long as I could convincingly play the part. As the ubiquitous ads for the Barbizon School explained, simply by sending away for their thirty-two-page booklet, I could train to be a model—or just look like one! I could actually be popular—or just tell myself I was!

My diary was not a place where I confessed all my most humiliating moments, a pink padlocked volume with *Keep Out!* scrawled on its first page. This book was a map for the woman I hoped to become, which required leaving out the embarrassments and disappointments.

And yet when I reread my diary now, the most making-of-me moments haunt the white space.

The Truth Will Set You Free

Hiya, Diary! I met this boy named Jeremy Pagano. He lives by Valerie. I think I like him. The other day he asked me, "Are you and Paul enemies or something?"

This opening sentence was soon after crossed out with a different pen, and under it I scrawled:

DISREGARD THIS ENTRY

Pay no attention to this story, Reader of the Future! Omit entirely from your memory that you did indeed like Jeremy Pagano, at least until he asked Paul what he thought of you, and Paul made it clear that Jeremy's first impressions were mistaken: you were in fact quite uncool, and flat-chested to boot. Which Jeremy Pagano then reported back to you. Remember exactly none of that, Future Self!

It was not only small mortifications which I attempted to excise entirely from memory. The more important a rite of passage, the more completely I dismissed it. In the entire diary, my changing body merits a single sentence:

I got it for the first time last month.

That day in Sister Angelique's math class, while taking a test, I felt something soaking the back of my stiff plaid uniform skirt. I remember sitting there, at first confused and then terrified. We didn't have sex education at St. Paul's, but I had read enough Judy Blume to know what was happening. But I was unsure how to get to the girls' lavatory without the whole class seeing for themselves. When I asked Sister Angelique whether I might be excused to go to the bathroom, she made me repeat myself more loudly. My cramps soon became so severe my mother had to come pick me up from the principal's office. At home I fended for myself with the mysterious supplies I'd discovered in a small cabinet at the bottom of our back stairs, hidden where only my mother might find and use them, and me too, when the time came.

But none of those pesky details were included in my record of that day. What I did include was an extensive scoring report of a basketball game featuring my school's team, the St. Paul Crusaders, handily beating Nativity of South Side.

I was not a basketball player. Our school had a girls' team, but back then the greater social currency by far was to wear saddle shoes and cheerlead for the boys' team, which really was special, even beyond the typical myopia of a grade-schooler. In Scranton, Pennsylvania, eighth-grade basketball games packed the bleachers and were covered extensively in the two daily newspapers. The St. Paul Crusaders were a perennial powerhouse. After an undefeated regular season and some easily won playoff games, our team—and the cheerleaders—won a trip to the Pennsylvania state championships in Johnstown.

In just fifty hours, the most exciting athletic event in my life will begin. Before that, there will be dances, parties, etc.! The bus there will be a six-hour trip that will be a total blast.

The mayor of Scranton came to see us off. On the bus ride we ate ham-and-cheese hoagies while the song "1999" blared repeatedly from Matt Camillo's boombox in the back. Per my diary, on that same ride it became known that Eric Benedetti liked Linda R., who said I could have him. I told her I didn't like him anymore. I did still like him, and found the idea that his attentions could skip right past my devotion to someone with Linda R.'s shrugging indifference temporarily devastating, but I saw no reason to tell my diary that. While the bus ride was not the "total blast" I had predicted, I believed what lay ahead still might be: staying in a hotel without my parents, competing against the cheerleaders from other schools, and screaming until I was hoarse.

In some ways it was everything I had hoped. Our team won the state championship in double overtime, with a memorably low final score of 29–27. I can still remember the ear-bursting excitement in that small, hot gym. I also remember being unable to jump around with the other cheerleaders because I was as sick as I'd ever felt in my life.

I was sick down in Johnstown, which was a BUMMER.

My vomiting, diarrhea, and fever commenced the first night in the hotel. I slept fourteen hours and missed the first two games. If there were dances and parties, I was not in attendance.

The only good thing was that it made me realize everyone cared.

The chaperones on the trip left Pepto-Bismol at my door and quickly reassigned my roommates.

It really showed me I had a lot of friends to count on.

By the end of that day those same "friends" had broadcast to all my peers that I had pooped in the bed and the whole room stank.

David Elkind also wrote that adolescents perceive themselves as having an "imaginary audience" of observers, people just as concerned with the minutiae of their behavior as the adolescents are themselves. In other words, teenagers think everyone else is talking about them, but this is merely a cognitive distortion.

In this case I fear that my audience may not have been entirely make-believe. No one teased me about my diarrhea shame that weekend—I must have been too visibly sick and pale for that to seem like much fun—but there was enough of a perimeter around me on the bus back to Scranton that my seat may as well have been marked off with crime-scene tape. I sat next to neither Jimmy Moloney nor Eric Benedetti, and by the time we got home I had missed entire eons, tectonic shifts in Who Likes Who while I was cold-sweating and contemplating a sweet death in the back row.

For the sake of my diary's imaginary audience—my future self—I transcribed none of this public disgrace. And some of it I have forgotten: all these years later, I can no longer recall exactly how the nausea and chills felt on that six-hour bus ride. But I can in an instant recall the humiliation and embarrassment I felt, crushed by the realization that all my careful curation of self had come to naught.

The Truth Will Set You Free

At least graduation was near, I told myself, and it gave me the sudden bravery that came from realizing I'd never be in the same place with all of these kids again anyhow. My middle school civilization, with its ironclad traditions and castes, was about to crumble away—to be immediately replaced by Central High School's own rules and hierarchies, sure, but that was still months away. Nothing mattered now but the dance that would take place in St. Paul's auditorium the night of our eighth-grade graduation ceremony.

I wore a white dress with a pink ribbon around its waist. Early in the evening I danced with three boys I didn't like. (According to my records, Jimmy Moloney did not number among them.) Soon, there was only one more slow dance. Our parents would be outside to pick us up in fifteen minutes.

Eric Benedetti seemed content hanging out by the snack table. I had to face it: he was never going to ask me to dance. On the other hand, at least he hadn't asked anyone else. But I couldn't wait any longer. Eric Benedetti was going to Scranton Prep. I might never see him again.

This was my last chance.

This was when I finally told my diary the truth about Eric.

> *I collected my nerves and tapped Eric on the shoulder. He turned around and said, "Huh? Hi."*
> *I said, "Hi. Want to dance?"*
> *He said, "Uh, okay."*
> *So we did, and it was G-R-E-A-T.*

Let's clear up a few things right now. I've been trying to kid myself saying what a jerk he is. He's nice. I like him. I suppose we've had a quiet thing going since seventh grade.

So quiet that Eric Benedetti went off to Scranton Prep with likely total unawareness that said "thing" had even occurred. But I got to feel his hand on the small of my back before we said goodbye.

I came back to my diary only once after that night—and then mostly to say that I probably wouldn't be back.

Monday, Jan 2nd
Here I am! Sorry I never write. But I've sorta given up on keeping a diary.
NEW YEAR'S RESOLUTIONS
Exercise for thirty minutes at least three times a week.
Tell people when I'm mad. Communicate. Don't keep it inside.
Try something new. (Skiing?)
Do everything I can to make the people I really love happy.

It is very me to have given myself a to-do list even as I bade farewell to this exercise of self-examination. And forty years later, the resolutions I give myself would remain pretty much the same. Forty years later, I haven't consistently achieved anything on that list.

If I'm the same after all these years, what does that say about me? Perhaps only that I already was then the person that I would become. That carefully editing out the mortifying things that happened during my adolescence was never going to help me become someone else.

David Elkind concluded that adolescent egocentrism passes, and the personal fable is overcome, "once the young person sees himself in a more realistic light." The older teenager comes to realize her experiences were not unique; she had only believed them to be so. Others, she learns, have suffered in the same way. Others have written diaries much like hers.

While I couldn't control what was happening to me in the year I kept my diary—let alone how it made me feel—I hoped that I might at least control what I would remember. And so I created an origin story for myself, as much a "real true diary" as *Go Ask Alice* had been. Only mine was the story of a girl who would grow up to live a full and happy life.

It didn't work. At least not in the way I intended. But my diary remains a gentle act of self-protection from the sadness and embarrassment and disappointments I experienced, which at least felt deeply formative to the thirteen-year-old personal fabler holding the pen. Amid all the ordering myself to be and do and become a better version of a teenage girl than I was, I was also showing kindness and gentleness to a person I loved—a person I really hoped would turn out okay.

Her life didn't have to be perfect. But when she looked back, she could think that it maybe almost was.

The Only One You Can Change Is You

Being called a perfectionist is the ultimate backhanded compliment. *You do it all so well! Just a little too well!* I admit I fit the profile: Virgo, handwriting with a consistent slant, regular flosser, health insurance IDs for my entire family saved on my phone. So for a long time, I had no problem with the term. It was a name a girl like me was supposed to call herself. Plus, self-identifying as a perfectionist can serve both as rueful admission and as a badge of honor. A humblebrag for a job interview.

Still, while I may have a high set point for achievement, I'm not obsessed with doing any of the things I do *perfectly*. My closet is a disaster, I leave texts on read for days, and I can sometimes walk right by the cushions and pillows strewn across my living room couch without stopping to fluff them. So I've come to resist being labeled as a perfectionist. I think it's too often a code word for "annoying." Yes, I'm extra, but I'm also the one people call when they're not sure what time the bus leaves for sleepaway camp.

If I were a perfectionist, that would mean there was something wrong with me.

Which, I now realize, sounds a lot like something a perfectionist would say.

I did have a phase where I called myself a "recovering perfectionist." That at least felt like witty shorthand for an overextended person who can laugh at her *former* neuroses. Flaws she for sure doesn't still have. But after a while "recovering perfectionist" didn't feel right either. I had never been someone afflicted by belief in my own deep inadequacy, unable to complete tasks, detesting the person I saw in the mirror. I was almost always a person who was too busy, but that was due to the literal circumstances of my life, not because I was cutting my kids' sandwiches into intricate shapes and triple-proofreading every email. What, exactly, was I recovering from?

And why were both "perfectionist" and "recovering perfectionist" both things men rarely called themselves?

Psychologists Paul Hewitt and Gordon Flett are considered the world's foremost experts on perfectionism. In the 1990s they defined its three subtypes: self-oriented, other-oriented, and socially prescribed. The "self-oriented" perfectionist is the familiar stereotype: a girl harboring excessive expectations for both her appearance and her grade point average, the one I was irked by any suggestion I might resemble. "Other-oriented" perfectionists also have extremely high standards, but for those around them more than for themselves. (Which might explain why Sister Benedicta was such a pill.)

And then there is the third type:

Socially prescribed perfectionism entails people's belief or perception that significant others have unrealistic standards for them, evaluate them stringently, and exert pressure on them to be perfect.

When I read about this third type a few years ago—the socially prescribed perfectionist—I thought, *Yes! Okay, yes. That's me.* It's not that I'm too hard on myself; it's that I'm struggling under the weight of the unrealistic societal standards to which all women are unreasonably held!

Then I noticed the "belief or perception" part. Those excessive requirements were being framed as subjective. From this scientific viewpoint, the world doesn't expect too much of women—we just *think* it does. In that case, making a change should be as easy as realizing we've only been imagining the feedback we receive at work that we sound too bossy, the idea that we're "letting ourselves go" if we go up a pants size, the daily assumptions that we know what our mother-in-law wants for Christmas and how to repaginate the presentation without losing all the column totals.

This whole time, the idea that we must do it all correctly—or at all—was but a figment of our collective imagination. And according to Hewitt and Flett, this misapprehension can cause the most dangerous sort of perfectionism by far: the socially prescribed perfectionist's attempts to meet those imaginary standards can lead to "severe levels of psychopathology."

Okay, then. I, for one, definitely do not think the world is harder on women. Forget I said anything.

Around the same time that perfectionism study was first published, when I was graduating from college and matriculating in the School of Life, there was this palm-sized book I'd always see stacked next to the cash register in gift shops and in airports: *Meditations for Women Who Do Too Much*. I was barely in my twenties, but I still got the joke. Ha! What woman *wouldn't* define herself as a woman who did too much? My great-great-grandmother, perhaps? Off to milk the cows at dawn, another day of farm labor ahead, Bridget Failey of County Cavan probably never stopped to consider whether her list was just too long. Whether things might be otherwise. Nothing she did was optional. There was no "me time" alternative to mucking out the stalls. She could never have imagined the life of her descendant entering adulthood a little more than a century later, a typically modern woman with a multitude of options and the overload of trying to have it all.

But *Meditations for Women Who Do Too Much* suggested that maybe that second part was the overwhelmed woman's own fault. It was not a book for women who had too much to do; it was for women who *did too much*. The book's title offered validation and blame in a single phrase, and in its pages author Anne Wilson Schaef offered 365 days of bite-sized reflections on all the problems the reader was unintentionally pulling to herself.

> *We women who do too much often see something that isn't working as a call to arms. We can work a little harder. Push a little harder. . . . Our holding on may make us sick.*

That the reader might make a different choice was presumed. Why didn't she? Schaef believed there was something within that frantic feeling that busy women claimed to resist and yet deeply desired, a panicked thrill such women were dysfunctionally drawn toward.

The Only One You Can Change Is You

Sometimes we even make tasks more complicated than they need be so we can keep busy. We feel safer when we are working. We get panicked with slack time.

There were no studies cited, no theories of developmental psychology underpinning these assertions. It was self-evident: some women were just like that, and the criticism these meditations offered was familiar enough to seem incontrovertible.

We workaholics are difficult to be around. . . . Our core form of functioning is control.

A woman's inability to relax was a thing of her own creation. To make matters worse, her resulting levels of stress made her a real drag to be around. The solution lay within: women who did too much needed to stop making their own lives so miserable.

Schaef's book was a huge bestseller. When I paged through it, as an adult-in-training, some of her ideas made hypothetical sense, although I wondered why these mindset shifts were required only of women. Weren't there men whose "core form of functioning" was control, whatever that meant? Weren't there men who did too much? It seemed to me that there were men who did enormous amounts, and always had been, but no one seemed to think that was *too* much; it was as it should be. Maybe their wives fretted about their blood pressure, but that was about it.

But as we were constantly reminded back then, men were Mars and women were Venus. We required different advice. We required different pH balances: as the deodorant commercials explained, Secret was strong enough for a man, but *made* for a woman. Of course the same rules didn't apply. If self-actualization for men meant getting ahead, self-actualization for women meant consuming a great deal of chicken soup for the soul.

I had begun cultivating my future adult self in earnest during my senior year of college, meeting my roommate back at our dorm room every weekday at four p.m. to unwind until the dining hall opened for dinner by watching *The Oprah Winfrey Show*. It was appointment television for us, a show we could both enjoy and feel good about watching. Never mind our constitutional law sections; we were learning just by sitting on our futon, getting actionable takeaways for our future female selves from the most powerful woman in the world.

Mind you, *Oprah* was also the only entertainment option available at that time of day on our bunny-eared, hand-me-down television, able to access exactly one broadcast channel. A college student today has one hundred million entertainment options, and even if she happened to choose an episode of *Oprah* out of everything available, she'd half-watch it in one of her six open browser tabs while simultaneously scrolling TikTok and group-texting with eight of her friends. I am glad I did not have to get through school with that level of distraction. But it did mean I came of age consuming what I watched without any snarky side commentary that made me question it. There were something like eleven episodes of *Scooby-Doo, Where Are You!* ever produced, and when I was a kid I watched each one about a hundred times, without ever wondering if I liked it, because that was what was on.

Until the dining hall opened for dinner, unless I wanted to

start studying, watching *Oprah* was all there was for me to do. That meant I gave it my full attention and internalized the lessons it offered uncritically.

Oprah had overcome incredible adversity on her path to riches and fame, and her show frequently featured guests facing their own obstacles, far more supersized than mine at the time, which were the senior thesis I wasn't writing—particularly on weekdays from four to five p.m.—and the fact that I was perilously close to zeroing out my beer-and-pizza account for the semester well ahead of schedule. But most of those guests, celebrities and regular folk alike, had succeeded in transforming their lives simply by setting the correct intentions. These happy endings were available to everyone equally. Julia Roberts always had a feeling that she would become famous, and then she did. And Rhonda S. from Lexington, Kentucky, found her dream job just by telling the universe she wanted it. It was scientific! If you weren't yet living your best life, the answers and solutions lay within. All you had to do was set a new goal, then manifest that belief into fruition.

The good news was that nobody was stopping you from achieving your wildest dreams! The bad news was the same: if you didn't get there, no one else could be to blame. But they didn't talk about that part as much. And even when Oprah interviewed people who still seemed pretty flawed and messy, it was clear there was still hope for them. If transformation hadn't occurred yet, they were blocked somehow, delaying their own success by selling themselves short.

Anne Wilson Schaef, author of *Meditations for Women Who Do Too Much*, had the fix. As she would explain on Oprah's show (and in the magazine that would later follow), women who felt stuck or overwhelmed needed to confront their universal underlying issue: codependence, a dysfunctional need to be needed. The burdens those women were struggling with were ones they, in their affliction, were unwittingly creating for themselves. The first step to changing their lives going forward would be to acknowledge how very unwell they had become.

If anyone were to deny that they were the problem, well, wasn't that just what an addict would do? And make no mistake, most of us were addicts: careoholics and shopaholics and chocoholics. In the recovery culture of the 1990s pretty much any noun could have "aholic" added to its end, making little linguistic sense if one stopped to consider it, but serving as a catch-all for anything that someone either did too much or loved too well.

To me, sitting there on the futon watching *Oprah* as a not-quite-adult, all that unhealthiness seemed like a trap that would be easy enough to avoid. Stop doing things that are dysfunctional! Start putting your own needs and desires first! There was no chance of my ever screwing that up. Watching *The Oprah Winfrey Show* every afternoon was like taking a daily emotional multivitamin to stave off unhappy grown-woman outcomes. I was setting the right intentions and manifesting the future I wanted. I'd never become a woman who did too much.

A woman who would look back and wonder how her life had gotten so off track.

Twenty-five years after those *Oprah*-watching afternoons, I left dinner waiting for the kids one night and walked to a church in our neighborhood, a building I had passed by hundreds of times

The Only One You Can Change Is You

without ever really taking stock of it. The sign taped to the main doors read simply *Fellowship*. I followed its arrow to a side entrance, then another handwritten sign to the lower level, for my very first Al-Anon meeting.

All I really knew that night was that this meeting was intended for anyone whose life had been affected by addiction. I supposed that included me, but only indirectly; I was going because someone I loved had asked me to attend these meetings in support of their recovery. I was pleased to have been given such a specific and supportive assignment. I assumed I would receive coaching on how to help people stay sober. Tips on what to watch for, ways to get better at helping. These were things I was eager to learn.

I did wonder whether I'd see anyone I knew. The population density of New York City usually offers a rough guarantee of anonymity in any group setting, but this was right in my own neighborhood. What if I saw someone I knew there? How uncomfortable that might be, me intruding on their privacy during a time of actual and immediate crisis, when my reason for being there would no doubt seem comparatively small.

I felt terrible I had missed the signs that my loved one was struggling. I felt guilty for not having done more to help sooner. Still, things already seemed much better, and if it helped knowing that I was attending these meetings, that was a good-person box I was more than happy to check. As I walked down those stairs, I was certain the hard part was over, certain I could accomplish whatever I was about to learn would be required to keep things on the right path.

At the bottom of the stairs I followed a final sign down the basement hallway, sure I knew where I was going even without it, planning how I would carefully qualify my attendance should I be obliged to speak. I'm fine, really, I would say. I'm mostly just here to listen.

This Way to the Solution!

I entered the room and found myself a seat among unfamiliar faces.

The meeting began with a reading.

We admitted we were powerless . . . that our lives had become unmanageable.

Wait. I was supposed to admit that for myself? *My* life had become unmanageable?

I'm looking for the meeting where you tell me how to help people. How did I end up in this room full of mirrors?

You're telling me *I'm* the one with the problem?

Here was the big takeaway that night: even if you manifest an intention not to become a sad, middle-aged lady with problems, you will probably become one anyhow.

Of course I deserved to be there. Of course I had problems. And I immediately remembered where I had heard some of these ideas before: the compulsion to control, the caretaking of others' needs in order to feel worthy. Codependence made a lot more sense here than it had on afternoon television, applied to men who just aren't that into you, or to those last few stubborn pounds. As I relearned at that meeting, this time nodding with increasing recognition, it was not my job to forever-fix everything for everyone in the world.

I thought of a breakfast I had just a few weeks earlier, at a diner just a few blocks from that church basement: a 7:30 a.m. meeting with the CEO of a performing arts organization in my role as vice-chair of its board. (My husband was handling the school drop-offs for a change.) This CEO had surprised me by asking me to join the theater's board after I brought the kids to its Saturday-morning performance series a handful of times. I had been flattered that this professional woman had seen me, then a messy mom of multiple toddlers, as someone who might have more to offer.

"You already do so much for us," the CEO said that morning at breakfast as our omelets were cleared from the table.

This is usually what people say right before they ask you to do more.

"But I'm hoping you'll consider becoming chair of the Fundraising Committee."

I was already serving on two of the board's other committees.

"I almost hate to ask," she added.

I didn't say anything for a moment. Agreeing to chair this third committee—the word "commit" was right in there, waving its red flag—would mean cold-calling donors and asking them to consider increasing their generosity. The very thought made me want to crawl into a hole.

"But it's just that you'd be marvelous at it," the CEO concluded. "And, really, who else is there?"

No one. There was no one else. The other board members had gravitas and gray hair and worked at law firms that had their own last names in their titles. I was a sometimes actor and writer and creative type, an all-the-time parent of three, who lived in the neighborhood and who set her own schedule. Wasn't I really the only one she could ask? And so while I had neither capacity nor interest for what was being asked of me, what was I supposed to say? *No*?

Yes. As I could now clearly see, that was exactly what I was supposed to have said. That everyone else had said no did not mean I was not allowed to do the same. I had only thought that others' refusal of this thankless task meant it therefore had to be mine.

"You know what they say," the CEO had said that morning, handing me a list of phone numbers as she signed for the check. "If you want something done, ask a busy person."

Here's what "they" should say: If you want something done, ask someone whose chief qualification is her inability to refuse.

In that church basement, I was being asked to consider that the people who can leave some of the hard things behind for someone else to handle might be *more* enlightened than me. Not less.

Admitting you have a problem isn't the solution, of course; it's the beginning of the work. Heaven knows I like a project, and what could be more important than a new way to fix myself? Not that I hadn't tried that before, ever since my days watching *Oprah*. While I hadn't chased every waterfall, I had followed the advice for overwhelmed women as it had shifted from "stop being a workaholic" to leaning in to #girlbossing it to washing my face to telling myself "You got this, Mama!" even when I most certainly did not. Good vibes only!

Whenever I heard about a new way I might be able to change, I would roll my eyes at first. Then the books would start stacking up on my nightstand again, the podcast episodes on my phone. Each new mindset shift promised relief, or at least a less-stuffed schedule. But what most of these approaches offered was less self-help than self-improvement. Every hallway doubled me back to that same room of mirrors.

This Way to the Solution!
You're the solution.
You're the problem.

Here's the thing I've finally learned about the power of letting go, the daring to lead, the life-changing magic of not giving a f*ck: no matter how much you tinker with your mindset, some of your problems are probably going to stick around.

Maybe that's okay. If we are meant to accept the things we cannot change, that means it is okay to leave those things alone. Even if they're not forever-fixed.

And that includes ourselves.

I stopped going to those church-basement meetings after about six months, not because they hadn't worked, but because they had. I didn't find an answer because there wasn't one, which gave me the freedom to stop looking for it. Plus, my loved one seemed happier. Or maybe that was just me.

But did the journey toward it have to be so freaking long?

If I could go back and advise the younger me manifesting an optimal future, could I have convinced myself that actualizing a life without problems didn't mean I wouldn't have any? That sometimes the things I struggled with would be exactly as hard as I thought they were?

Can I save myself any time now by confessing to being, after all, a woman who does too much? Who overcomplicates things needlessly? Who still wonders whether there's a magical solution out there somewhere?

Probably not. You can't collapse a timeline. Recovery is, as they say, a lifelong process.

Never Give Up

When my three children were still small it was easy to imagine myself as the leader of all our family adventures, then and in the future that would come. I knew where we all were going and how we would get there. If they beat me across the pool, it was because I was letting them win.

I think kids are often aware of this tacit arrangement, and they like it that way. With so much in their lives existing in the quadrant of the Unknown Unknown, the bad things they don't even know about yet, children are usually content to have a grown-up there to hold their hand or tell them how high they're allowed to climb. That they can scooter just to the corner, and then they have to stop and wait for Mommy. It was easy to appear brave in my children's eyes; it was easy to *feel* brave when everything we did together seemed predictable and familiar.

That all changed the winter that I was forty and my children were between the ages of three and seven: the winter that my young children and I learned to ski.

Despite having grown up an hour from the Pocono Mountains, despite telling myself I should take up the sport in my eighth-grade diary, I'd gotten to midlife without ever having put on skis. It just wasn't something my family did. Neither of my parents knew how to ski. Nor did the speech-and-debate types I hung out with in high school. But my husband—who grew up just two miles from where I did—went to a different high school, one that offered no-frills twenty-dollar ski-club trips to Elk Mountain on Friday nights. He and his friends skied in jeans and had a ball.

"You taught *yourselves*?" I asked. It seemed a little more complicated than that, but what did I know.

"It's easy," he said. "You'll see. Everyone will get the hang of it in a day, and then we can all ski together for years. We'll be making memories."

On this we fervently agreed—if the kids would have fun doing it, it was worth our doing. Whether my husband or I got a thrill out of touching trucks or doing the corn maze at Pumpkintown was beside the point: our children enjoyed those things, so those were the things we did. I didn't exactly love the idea of adding an athletic activity to that mix, but that was for historical and personal reasons. Anything involving speed or strength or throwing or catching has always existed far outside my comfort zone. If you want to ruin my month, just tell me our next outdoor gathering will include a friendly volleyball game. And I've never needed the exhilaration of risk or danger to make my life more exciting. I'll go on the roller coaster, but I'll keep my hands inside the ride at all times.

But I wanted my kids to have a slightly more carefree relationship to adventure than that, so in service of that end, I needed to step up and be Fun Mom. This was a low-stakes way for me to challenge the scaredy-cat within. I would show my children how richly rewarding it was to try something new. I wouldn't be waving gaily to my menfolk from the back door, then wiping my hands on my apron as I watched them set off without me. I would be right there, participating in the family fun. There was even a good chance, my husband told me, that I'd become the skier in the family.

That first day on the bunny slope, the scariest part was getting off the lift at the top of the hill. "Bend your knees, lean forward just a little, let the seat push you," my husband told me before heading off to the kids' area with the boys. It took me several tries to do it without the attendant having to pause the lift to assist me, but I could accept that embarrassment because the part that I expected to be hard—the skiing part—was going great! I'd just tip myself over the edge of the hill, balance myself over my skis, feel about ten seconds of exhilaration, then have about forty feet of nice flat terrain to bring me to a gradual and gentle stop.

After about thirty times down, I thought I was Lindsey Vonn, thrilling to the feeling of the wind in my hair. Part of the lightness I felt may have been that my kids weren't with me. I hoped the boys were enjoying themselves as much as I was! I couldn't wait to see my family again and tell them I had done it. I hadn't fallen once. It seemed I was an athlete and adventurer after all.

The following weekend we returned to the same ski mountain, just me, my husband, and our first grader. (Our younger two kids stayed home with my in-laws so the three of us could really shred.) As soon as my seven-year-old and I were booted up and strapped in, I started push-striding back to the bunny slope.

"No, this way!" my husband said, calling me toward a different, longer lift line. "We're going to do a *real* hill!"

I tried to ignore my immediate feeling of dread. This was exactly why I hated being adventurous: as soon as you feel comfortable, people want you to ratchet up the level of risk. *I'm not ready*, I wanted to protest. *Let's do the bunny slope some more.* But my first grader was the opposite of frightened, yelling "C'mon, Mom!" as he trudged toward the line on his little skis.

If my little boy wasn't scared, then why was I? If Dad said we were ready, then we definitely were, and so a "real hill" was what was going to happen next. I had my qualms, but I got in line. All I needed to do was get over my fears, and then? It was going to be so much fun.

While I was not aware of this at the time, the Professional Ski Instructors of America strongly recommend that new skiers take a few lessons—from a licensed and bonded instructor—before they attempt any sort of actual hill. Self-taught is insufficient, and whomever you came with probably isn't a good enough teacher either; as they explain on their website, "Friends don't let friends teach friends."

If a Professional Ski Instructor of America is not available to you, then experts say it might be possible to learn from a non-professional. In a pinch, you might be able to learn a few tips from any number of competent strangers you encounter in the lift line. But under no circumstances, according to our nation's professional ski instructors, should one learn to ski from one's spouse—even if said spouse *is* a Professional Ski Instructor of America. To teach a romantic partner to ski is a mistake experienced instructors know to avoid, because such a heightened and anxiety-provoking forum makes yelling a far more likely outcome than learning. And for the new skier herself, learning from the person closest to her offers an additional risk: that her loved one's relationship-based nearsightedness might cause him to overlook that he has brought his life partner to the top of a ski run without her knowing two important things.

How to turn.

And how to stop.

As soon as the three of us reached the top of the hill that afternoon—a green run called "Easy Street"—my seven-year-old took off. Without fear. Without *poles*, which is how kids ski, probably because it appears much more dangerous to their mothers that way. I hadn't seen my child skiing until this moment, and his lack of hesitancy was the opposite of reassuring.

"Wait!" I yelled. It seemed to me he was going far too quickly, his little red helmet already barely visible in the distance.

"He's got this," my husband said. "Look at him go! Okay, you ready?" He gestured for me to proceed. "Ladies first!"

As I stood looking down this precipitous drop, unable to see either my child or the bottom of the hill, I began to sense my spouse had perhaps made an error in judgment.

"I don't know what I'm doing," I said, frozen in place.

"Sure you do!" my husband said.

I didn't move.

"Okay!" he said. "No problem!" although I could see he was rapidly recalibrating his own expectations. "We'll do this together, okay? We're going to work our way across the hill sideways. Good. Keep your toes pointed in. Nice and sl—"

I didn't hear anything he said after that, because as soon as I moved from where I had been frozen in place, I was suddenly flying down the hill, also at top speed.

"Snowplow! *Snowplow!*" my husband was yelling behind me, which would have probably been a helpful suggestion if I had any idea what "snowplow" meant, or how one might perform such a maneuver.

Then I could hear him yelling, "Not french fries! *Pizza!*" and that I could translate: he was telling me to form a triangle with my skis. I'd seen other people doing that on the bunny slope and wondered why they were going so slowly. *This isn't even scary!* I had thought, whizzing past them on the ten percent incline. *What losers.*

Now, as I whizzed down this much longer and steeper slope, I was unable to redirect my skis from their dread purpose. My skis were in charge, and both were pointed directly downhill.

As I passed the speed of sound, I tried to remember what people who knew how to ski looked like when they were skiing. The best example my mind's eye could muster was the "Agony of Defeat" guy from *Wide World of Sports.* Bending my knees, I crouched down just like him, which had the predictable but unfortunate effect of making me go even faster.

I knew I was in danger. If I couldn't slow down, I definitely had to stop. Just before I spectacularly faceplanted, I managed to tuck sideways and throw myself down next to a tree.

My husband skied up behind me. "Everything's going to be fine," he said, although I could tell that his miscalculation of my abilities now seemed as grave to him as it did to me. "Let's get up," he added, rather optimistically, since I had no idea how to do that either, and I was intending to cling to precious life by lying there in that snowbank for as long as possible.

Then I realized: if my seven-year-old had reached the bottom of the run without grave injury—which now seemed by no means a foregone conclusion—my little boy was down there all alone right now, wondering where his parents were, getting more frightened by the moment.

I started scrambling around in the snow, my husband hoisting me up by my armpits. "Hold on!" he said. "Your skis are pointing—"

Downhill. *Got it*, I thought as I accelerated away from safety once more.

That was how I made it down the mountain that day: achieving dangerous speed for about twenty seconds at a time, then dumping myself off to the side just before I tore an ACL, then waiting for my husband to assist me back up onto my skis while I shouted at him that this was all his fault. It was imagining my son's peril that was really fueling my panic. I wouldn't let my first grader take off alone at Disney World, or anywhere else, for that matter, so why was this considered acceptable on a ski slope? If someone were going to kidnap a child, didn't the bottom of a ski hill offer the most obvious of bounties?

Finally, amid a full-blown anxiety attack, I lay there in the snow and told my husband I was done. He would have to go ahead without me, first to find our son, then to commandeer a snowmobile to come get me. In response my husband gently suggested that the ski mountain's rescue teams were probably not usually dispatched to the bottom half of a hill they had named "Easy Street."

We somehow made it safely to the bottom, just twenty-five minutes behind our son. And there he was, waiting for us, gazing hopefully uphill in his red helmet. "Well, I was a *little* worried," he admitted. "I was *starting* to be." But with just a few tater tots in the lodge, he was set nicely back to rights. I, on the other hand, was thoroughly traumatized, and swore, nursing my tepid foam cup of Swiss Miss, that I would never, ever strap on those viselike boots again.

On the next snowy Saturday morning, when I stayed in my

HAPPY TO HELP

pajamas, my child said that he preferred to do the same. His younger brother, always happy to do whatever his older sibling did, said he didn't want to go skiing either. Everyone was happy about this except my husband. "You can't just *quit*!" he said after pulling me out of earshot of our children.

I explained that I was doing just that: while I took a grim pride in having survived the worst, I would not be heading back to Easy Street in this lifetime.

"But—if you don't go, the boys won't want to go either!" he protested.

This, too, was fine with me; skiing was far too dangerous an activity for any sensible person to consider. But my husband was not about to abide three quitters in one family.

"Okay, I know that was rough," he said, "but it won't always be like that. Which is exactly why you can't stop now! You can't let *that* have been your last skiing experience." He assured me that I'd enjoy it far more if I gave it another shot. Maybe took a lesson this time. He promised me that it really would click and fall into place, that skiing would turn into Great Fun. All I had to do was keep going. All I had to do was allow our nonrefundable plane tickets to Utah, rather than my fears, define what was possible.

Two months later, there I was, staggering across the snows of the West in boots of lead to drop our three-year-old daughter off for her own first lesson, on a hill so barely a hill they called it "Candy Land." Independent and fearless since birth, my youngest child headed off with a friendly goggled stranger and a half dozen of her peers without so much as a backward glance. My husband had already taken our two sons for their own lesson, after my having insisted they be properly trained in the lifesaving "Snowplow" and "Pizza" methodologies, while I would have two hours' instruction of my own. By then I'd be "having a ball," my husband assured me, as I wrestled three young children into long underwear and ski pants.

I had specifically requested I be matched with a teacher who had compassion for the reluctant adult ski-learner. My instructor turned out to be a windburned, wizened older man named Tex, who was transparently less than thrilled to be spending the morning with such a fraidy-lady.

As we began, I was mostly distracted by the presence of my preschooler. Since I had termed myself a "True Beginner," Tex and I were also hanging out on Candy Land, right next to her. Out of the corner of my eye she learned to ski a hula-hoop obstacle course as I knock-kneed it down Candy Land with none of her finesse.

Tex was disgusted. "Try having a little fun!" he said. "Come on, now. You haven't smiled at all yet."

This was true, but only because gritting my teeth was a crucial component of my new skiing method, which had evolved from "Brace for Impact" to something more like "Maximize Drag Coefficients." I had learned how to lock my skis into a pizza shape and zigzag across Candy Land painfully slowly. I was in a full sweat from the considerable effort both to slow my skis and to avoid collision with the forty freestyling toddlers paying absolutely no heed to where they were going—which is admittedly what they usually do, just at lower speeds.

"Well, okay, then," Tex said. "We'll go up just a little higher. Get away from all the kids, if they're distracting you."

He was doing his best to chitchat and keep me moving forward. "Now, remind me how many kids you have?" he asked, as our legs dangled off the chair lift.

"I'm—I just—uh—three." The chair lift hadn't been as high off the ground in the Poconos. I craned my neck looking downhill for my daughter, wondering how many collisions on Candy Land had occurred due to inattentive skiers dropping from above.

"What are you so worried about?" Tex said. "Relax! Enjoy the view!"

I was gripping the handrail for dear life. "I'm sorry," I admitted. "It's just—I'm really scared right now."

"You're afraid of *this*?" Tex snorted. "This itty-baby chair lift?"

Yes, Tex, I wanted to say. *Yes, I am, and your ridicule is making me feel so much better about that.* The chair lift was frightening, and so was the rapidly approaching dismount ahead. All of this was frightening. None of this was fun.

My phone buzzed in my pocket. After Tex saw me safely off the chair lift, I paused to see who had texted me. It was my husband, letting me know that our five-year-old had just skied his first black diamond.

It was me. It wasn't skiing—it was me. If my five-year-old could master a mountain in two and a half hours, then I needed to get over myself. *When things get hard, we push through*, I told myself. *We conquer the dragon, and we emerge holding the Gleaming Chalice of Grit.*

I redoubled my efforts, and by the time I bid farewell to Tex an hour later, I had learned to turn (by jerkily skidding on the tilted edges of my skis) and to stop (by leaning my body uphill while praying). My husband and three children, ready to meet

Never Give Up

me for lunch at the bottom of the hill, watched my shaky, final approach.

"Yay, Mommy!" my five-year-old shouted. "Now we can all ski together!"

I managed a smile, but only because I had earned an hour off the mountain, or at least the time it took until everyone's chicken nuggets were finished.

After lunch it was time for Forced Family Skiing. I rode the chair lift with my seven-year-old to the top of Little Baldy. Nothing about it felt "Little" to me, but my oldest child's enthusiasm was infectious.

"You're going to have so much more fun higher up the mountain, Mom!" he yelled. "Because the hill is way longer!"

"But, sweetheart, I don't *want* the hill to be longer," I said. "Every time I get to the bottom of Candy Land I can't believe I didn't hurt myself. How many times did you ski before you stopped being afraid?"

My child regarded me blankly.

This was the same child that I'd had to repeatedly reassure, just a few years earlier, that there was absolutely no way the Grumpy Old Troll was going to harm Dora the Explorer, let alone him. "The Grumpy Old Troll isn't even mean!" I would explain. "His riddles are in no way dangerous! Look at him! He's just *grumpy*!" But I could see in my child's eyes that he was beyond convincing. It was of minimal solace that his mother, for whatever reason, couldn't see what was so clearly unsafe.

Two hours later, I still hadn't fallen. I had even smiled a few times skiing some basically horizontal greens with my three-year-old while my older kids did moguls and tree runs (whatever those were). With the longest day of my life almost behind me, all that remained between me and the parking lot was a green run—I could do those now!—named, encouragingly, "Success."

"Come on, Mom!" my older son yelled. "Catch up with us, and we'll all finish together!"

The sun was getting lower in the sky, and the snow was slushy. A crunchy layer of ice was forming on top, making a scraping sound against my skis that I was trying to ignore. And when we came around the bend, the steepest hill I had seen yet was before me. Whoever had named this hill "Success," and deemed it a green run, had long ago lost touch with what a new skier might perceive as easy. The mountain was covered in ice, packed with skiers racing to the rental return, and far, far beyond my capability.

There was nowhere to go but down. I had never been—still have never been—so afraid in my life.

"Leave me alone!" I screamed at my husband when he tried to coach me through my panic. As I watched my children fly down ahead of me, I was scared for them, exhausted for me, and ashamed. I was all wrong. I carved my way down the mountain in a painfully slow zigzag, no longer caring if anyone thought I was brave. I was certainly not. I had survived Success, but with none of the happiness my children felt, none of the joy they had only wanted to share with me.

If those who can't, teach, then I'd be a heck of a ski instructor. Here's what I'd tell my students:

It's harder to go down the hill slowly than it is to go quickly.

If you don't fall once in a while, you won't get any better.

If your hands hurt from gripping the poles, you're holding on too tightly.

And, most important: it's way more fun to be fearless.

I held all these truths to be self-evident. I simply could not apply their wisdom to myself. And how was I ever going to catch up to my children? They were already growing impatient with me, already telling me to go faster, already exhibiting freewheeling skills I wasn't sure I could ever approximate. Our experiences were already too different. It was already too late.

I told all of this to my husband under the covers that night, knowing he'd tell me what I needed to hear: to keep going, even though I didn't want to, because I had to, because I needed to, because beating the things that scare us is how we grow.

And then, just before he turned off the light, my husband said, "Well. You don't have to keep doing this, you know. Maybe you just quit."

People who truly love to ski love skiing more than just about anything else. On the mountain they achieve what psychologist Mihaly Csikszentmihalyi famously termed a "flow state," a complete, adrenaline-fueled absorption that is something close to bliss. "The best moments in our lives are not the passive, receptive, relaxing times," Csikszentmihalyi wrote. "The best moments usually occur if a person's body or mind is stretched to its limits in a voluntary effort to accomplish something difficult and worthwhile."

In the service of Future Flow, in the service of never, ever giving up, I might have spent many more frightening afternoons locking those heavy boots onto my feet and staring down Success. Perhaps I was almost to the other side, about to accomplish something difficult and therefore worthwhile. I will never know, because while I skied one more day after that—and discovered, as the sun set over Baldy Mountain, that I still hated it—I have delighted in the freedom of never going back.

If getting good at something is hard, being good at something is easy. Had I kept at it, the story might have ended where it feels like it should: with my feeling the exhilaration of freedom, instead of the ridiculous fear that Tex and my first grader were unable to comprehend. But instead of overcoming my anxiety, I overcame my fear of stopping, which held a euphoria even better than getting good at skiing: the joy of accepting my limitations and weaknesses as forever unfixable.

I wanted to like skiing because my husband and children loved it, because it felt like I'd be disappointing them if I stopped. I wondered what had changed my husband's mind, that quitting might not be so terrible. Then I wondered why I hadn't allowed myself to change my own mind first. We don't have to keep doing things we hate until someone else gives us permission to put them down.

My kids still ski, of course, because they love it, and because they take their safe arrival at the bottom of the mountain for granted. While I wait for them at the bottom, I tromp around in the snow, I read by the fire, and not even a small part of myself feels guilty for not joining them. My quitting affected my children far less than I had feared. Skiing with me was only slowing them down. As my children grew, they stopped looking furtively at me to see whether the Grumpy Old Troll was dangerous, whether Donald Duck was approachable, whether it was okay to try something new. As my children continue to grow, what their mother would do in any given situation is about the last thing they take into their personal risk consideration.

This is exactly as it should be. If I've taught my children anything really useful, it's that saying "no" can sometimes be its own kind of bravery. Hoping we don't get hurt is no kind of a way to live.

First, Do No Harm

The medieval friar and philosopher William of Ockham had some ideas that got him in trouble. In the early 1300s he told the pope that his ownership of property and opulent lifestyle made him a heretic. Ockham caused further scandal by explaining that, while God became incarnate as Jesus Christ, He might also have chosen to come to Earth as a donkey. Or as both at the same time.

But Ockham's most lasting and influential idea—at least as ascribed to him in the centuries since—is *Entia non sunt multiplicanda praeter necessitatem*. "Entities should not be multiplied beyond what is necessary." Or, as our more modern philosophers might put it: don't make things more complicated than they need to be.

These days "Occam's razor"—the "k" in Ockham disappearing somewhere along with the widespread usage of Latin—is invoked to suggest that the simplest explanation for an event is the one most likely to be true. The "razor" trims away all assumptions, all that is hypothetical and irrelevant, leaving only what is most factual and basic. I'm no High Middle Ages theologian, but when faced with uncertainty, I have always found comfort in focusing on what I know for sure.

This probably explains why I wasn't alarmed the day my first grader passed out, even though I was standing right behind him when it happened.

I was one of several parent chaperones that day on a field trip to the New York City Fire Museum. As a retired firefighter explained the anachronistic function of a nineteenth-century hand pumper, I saw my child start to sway. He slumped right into the antique machine and slid down to the ground.

My child's classmates gathered around to see what would happen next, as this was far more interesting than any old fire engine. My child looked cozily asleep there on the floor, so sweet I almost hated to wake him. The kids had all been wearing their winter coats inside. Of course this was going to happen to one of them. If I was certain of anything in that moment, it was my own stupidity for not having thought to take my son's jacket off.

My child was already coming around, blinking in confusion.

"I'll call 911. I'm assuming you'll want to ride with him to the hospital," one of the teachers said, pulling out her cell phone.

"God, please no. No ambulance!" I said.

"But—that's school policy," she explained. "I have to call an ambulance for any sort of serious medical event."

I gestured to the bench where my child had been carried. One retired first responder was checking his pulse. Another had gotten him some Gatorade, for the salt. His fellow first-graders were looking on in envy and awe.

"I think he's getting the attention he needs," I said.

"You good, little buddy?" another avuncular firefighter asked.

When my son nodded, the teacher admitted that my parental presence, along with that of several CPR-trained professionals, meant a ride to the hospital with sirens blaring might not be strictly necessary. *Thank God I was right there to prevent her from calling 911*, I thought. An ambulance was the last thing he needed. Otherwise, my child might have been very frightened.

We did, however, skip the school bus ride back uptown. My son was sleepy in the taxi and wanted to lie down in his bed as soon as we got home. While he slept, I checked in with his pediatrician; the fainting plus the long nap seemed like something I should at least let her know about.

"Glad you called me," she said, "but, yeah, kids faint. And like you said, it was hot in there. Unless it happens again, there's really no reason for concern."

This was why I loved this doctor—she was as disinclined to dramatic conclusions as I was. Nothing to see here.

On a Saturday morning two weeks later, my son didn't come to the kitchen when I yelled that his pancakes were ready. I gave the other two kids theirs, then went around the apartment looking for him. This was a child who could become so deeply absorbed in his toys or video games that he didn't hear you calling, even when it was pancakes you were yelling about. Expecting to find my child lost in the fantasy land of Monstro City on the desktop in the den, I was, admittedly, preparing to lose my patience. Instead, I found him unconscious on the floor. He was breathing, and he didn't seem to have hit his head when he fell, but when I shook him he was unresponsive.

My other kids ran in when they heard me yelling their brother's name. I told them to go get their dad, holed up in our bedroom on a conference call, an interruption usually strictly prohibited. My husband came out of the bedroom, mouthing *I am on the phone!* Then he stopped, his face as white as our child's, whose eyes were by now open, although he still seemed pretty out of it.

"I was picking a wallpaper for my Moshi Monster's room, and then I felt *really* worried," he said. "Like something bad was going to happen. But then I said to myself, it's okay. You don't have to be worried. Because nothing bad happens in Moshi Monsters."

His pediatrician thought we should run a few tests. Just to rule things out.

Later that week I watched as a neurologist's assistant attached electrodes to my child's skull while he chattered about the methods of evolution of various Pokémon. I gave his monologue my full attention, thankful he remained distracted from the whole process, that he couldn't see how bonkers he looked with a dozen wires attached to his little head. The printer alongside him was presenting a series of wavy lines, a reading of his brain waves that looked like the lie detector tests you see on TV. Only these lines weren't jumping around crazily, revealing the internally itchy conscience of the true killer. These lines were a picture of my seven-year-old's brain, and they looked nice and flat and regular to me. It would certainly rule out whatever it was we were here for, and then solving these "syncopal episodes," as the pediatrician was now calling them, was probably just a matter of increasing the potassium in my child's diet.

That was what I was still thinking as we were called to the neurologist's office twenty minutes later. My child sat there next to me in a chair that left his feet dangling off the floor.

"The EEG shows clear centrotemporal spikes in the left anterior quadrant," the doctor explained, pointing to what he seemed to think were unmistakable signs in the readout. "Your child has epilepsy. Those two recent losses of consciousness were seizures."

I could feel my child's eyes on me, trying to calculate his mother's reaction to the doctor's big words. I froze, the icy realization washing over me that the improbable thing we had come here to exclude was, in fact, what was happening.

"You're going to want to start medication tonight," the neurologist explained with extra calm, probably seeing in my face that he now had two people at risk for a syncopal episode right there in his office. "Having two seizures in such close succession puts him at imminent risk for a third."

I tried to process what the doctor was saying. My child was in danger, right at that moment. He had been in danger for some time, the signs perfectly clear, and me not taking them nearly seriously enough. But that was only because I hadn't known, I told myself, taking deep breaths in through my nose and out through the mouth, keeping a smile on my face as my child looked on. Starting now, I would do everything in my power to keep my child safe.

My husband returned my panicked phone call while I was hustling my child across Lexington Avenue to get to the pharmacy before it closed. I spoke to him in code, holding our child's hand and looking both ways, explaining that, yes, our child had something called epilepsy, wasn't that interesting? And it was something the doctor said might make your brain give you funny feelings sometimes, or could even make you fall down! But it was definitely, totally going to be fine, because the medicine we were on our way to get would taste just exactly like bubble gum.

HAPPY TO HELP

Childhood epilepsy with centrotemporal spikes is most frequently diagnosed in boys between the ages of six and eight, just as my son had been. It is believed to be genetically determined. More often than not, it's a type of epilepsy that's outgrown by puberty, although hearing that when your child is seven is of colder comfort.

Seizures caused by epilepsy are like electrical storms in the brain, sometimes almost imperceptible and sometimes causing convulsions or—in my child's case—losses of consciousness. While frequent seizures can cause brain damage or sometimes even death, a seizure is not usually dangerous in and of itself.

It is secondary injury that's the true risk.

My son had already needed stitches four times in his young life, and they had usually happened for reasons we couldn't explain, even if we were right there when the injuries occurred. He'd be standing right there next to you, then he'd somehow have fallen to the floor, hitting his head on the kitchen counter or coffee table as he fell. Once I was summoned to the childcare room at the gym to find my then three-year-old with torn ear cartilage, a distraught babysitter acknowledging she had seen him hit his head on the edge of a round play table, but also swearing she had no idea what could possibly have caused him to fall.

The lack of clarity around these events was frustrating, but the simplest explanation was the most likely: our little tough guy played hard, and he was just accident-prone. We joked about it with the plastic surgeon we'd seen more than once in the same emergency room. He reassured us, after telling our son the story of Goldilocks and the Three Bears while stitching up his ear, that some kids were just repeat customers.

Now these past injuries all made new and terrible sense. While it was scary to consider what could have happened, we now had the certainty we needed to move forward. We knew now how to keep our child safe. That meant the bad part was behind us.

I dwelled in this sense of comfort for about ten days until my child, in the middle of a tantrum beyond anything I'd ever seen, threw a coffee mug across the room. A coffee mug that still had coffee in it.

"That is not who he is," I told the neurologist when he called me back. "He is just not a kid who would do something like that. Could this be a side effect of the new medicine?"

"Not at that tiny dose, no," the doctor said, saying it was more likely that the behavioral issues were a side effect of the epilepsy itself, although we could certainly try a different medication.

The second medication had to be discontinued after a few days because it caused a dangerous rash. With a third medication, the rash disappeared but the tantrums worsened. The cold-turkey removal of that third medication necessitated a hospital stay for observation and treatment of the seizure activity we were told would undoubtedly occur when the preventative medication was so suddenly removed. The doctors would be able to monitor that activity and get more information. Then we'd understand what was happening. Then we'd have more answers.

After two days of our child tethered to continuous EEG monitoring, playing Uno and painting with watercolors as dozens of wires sprang from his head, we were told that there must have been a mistake. Our child's EEG was completely normal, without any seizure activity at all.

The neurologist who had diagnosed him with epilepsy gaped at these new readouts while other doctors explained that some seizures were in reality expressions of deep psychological distress, just like tantrums. When we explained that our child had only started behaving that way since starting anti-seizure medication, we were asked to consider whether our child had suffered a trauma of which we were unaware. We were given a referral for parental counseling. One resident advised that when our child had a tantrum we should confine him to his bedroom, holding the doorknob from the outside so he could not escape. After I questioned the wisdom and basic humanity of that approach, he handed us our discharge papers, wishing all of us luck.

We took our child home while I struggled to create a new explanation for it all. Only one thing had changed over the last six weeks, and it wasn't my parenting approach—it was the addition of mood-altering medications. Ones it now seemed my child might not have needed in the first place. And now that we knew all the increased activity could not have been caused by a neurological disorder, it must have been caused either by those medications or by my child's fear of an ongoing medical ordeal, or both. In either case, it was a situation that I had helped create as his parent. All other assumptions had been stripped away. There was nothing wrong with my child. There was something very wrong with me.

A few weeks later, my child came and found me, his eyes wide with fear. "I can't move my mouth!" he tried to say, but couldn't: half his face was frozen. At first, I assumed he was just being dramatic, trying to get sympathy after another tussle with his older brother. Then my stomach dropped into my shoes as I realized this was a hemifacial seizure, a telltale sign of centrotemporal

First, Do No Harm

epilepsy no one had ever mentioned in my child's presence. This was not a hypothetical; it was evidence. It was happening after all. It was real.

I took him for another EEG, and after a couple of weeks off medication, there was more evidence still: the centrotemporal spikes were back. The first doctor had been right. My child had epilepsy, after all.

I ordered him a dog-tag medical necklace to start wearing under his clothes. There was a cost to that, a sick-kid message my kid would encounter anew each morning. But he could have a seizure at any time, and what if I wasn't right there? We had to do everything we could to protect him, including beginning a trial of a fourth medication, now that we knew seizure activity was occurring. All we could do was hope for fewer side effects, although whatever might come to pass would be part of the bargain for keeping him safe. Choosing not to medicate—to do nothing—was never presented to us as a possibility. Nor was it an option we ever considered. When the strange events continued, when our child would suddenly go pale or pass out, the doctors would concur that the medicine wasn't working. Then they would explain that it was because he needed to be taking more of it.

The doctors were in less agreement when it came to exactly what was wrong. Epilepsy can present in many ways, but some of what was occurring didn't match even its broadest profile. My child was lightheaded and disoriented. He'd sit down on the floor in the middle of math class and then ask his teacher how he'd gotten there. He'd fall asleep in the cafeteria or on a stranger's shoulder on the M104 bus. Doctors performed blood work and MRIs and tilt-table tests. Everything looked great: his blood sugar, his vitamin B_{12}, his fractionated catecholamines. No one could figure out why he was having these "brown-outs." They were not what we had seen before—not losses of consciousness—they were just some sort of altered state.

"Your child is fascinating," one doctor told me after another round of testing proved robustly ordinary. "I mean, you hate to tell a parent that, but it's true." Seeing from my expression that my own feelings about the situation were a tad less detached, the doctor then hastened to remind me of the long list of bad things that had been ruled out. All we had to go on was epilepsy, and his subtype was both common and relatively benign.

I knew she was right. I knew I should take comfort in all that had been pared away and live in the most-of-the-time that my kid was just fine. But my son's safety had become the spinning beach ball in the corner of my screen, sabotaging my entire operating system. Two years after he had fainted at the museum he had cold sweats almost every day, nausea, long stretches where he could do nothing but sleep. When we went to the school Christmas concert and saw our son take his place in the middle of the top bleacher, I wanted to scream, *Get him down from there! He could pass out at any moment!* But he'd get through the concert just fine. Another quiet week or two would go by, and I'd resolve to leave him alone, not one more appointment or test.

The next day my phone would buzz in my pocket. "He's fine," the school nurse would say as soon as I picked up. "He's here with me, he's fine." And then: "You better come get him. It happened again."

"I'm probably crazy for asking, but is there any chance it's the medication?" I asked the next neurologist we met with. This doctor was the head of the department at a hospital in the Bronx;

we'd waited months for this appointment so I could get his second (okay, fourth) opinion.

"I've never, in thirty years, seen a patient have such a reaction," he said. "Such a reaction would be extremely rare." Weird things were happening, things that couldn't be completely explained by an abnormal EEG, but since they did not seem to be dangerous, it was professionally preferable not to offer an explanation. Assuming nothing meant doctors could allow his condition to remain unexplained and send us home without troubling afterthought.

But this was my child. And his third-grade teacher had called to tell me that while she could manage to get him through the end of the school year, she wasn't sure fourth grade was going to work out unless things improved.

Something was very wrong.

I knew the last thing I should do, when I took my son to see these specialists, was seem frustrated or overly solicitous. It was important I choose my follow-up questions carefully, pose them breezily. *No, of course! Obviously, what did I know? I was just wondering.* I needed to seem well informed but not too much so, lest these doctors begin to suspect whether what was occurring for my child, based on his reports and mine, was happening at all.

Whether the real problem might be me.

⁓

Almost all documented cases of Munchausen syndrome by proxy are of a mother toward a child. These days it's usually called factitious disorder imposed on another (FDIA), a more accurate name for the deliberate deceit and abuse that is at cause. Healthcare providers are taught to suspect FDIA whenever a child is mysteriously and seriously ill. Further red flags include whether the patient's mother seems medically knowledgeable, whether the symptoms reported by the mother are observed in clinic, whether the mother seems almost *too* cooperative, and whether her levels of worry seem intense.

Judging by these criteria, I knew there should already have been a hit Lifetime movie based on the true story of my capture and trial.

I showed up for each appointment with a laptop full of details, a suspiciously complete understanding of various classes of anti-convulsants, and a kid who had never had one of these strange episodes while under medical supervision. But what mother of a mysteriously ill child wouldn't chase specialists, show up with lists of questions, and research the disorders that might be worth consideration?

On the other hand, why wouldn't that investment and concern be seen by some medical professionals as potentially suspect, especially when they are out of other ideas about what else could be happening?

It's unthinkable that there are mentally ill parents who make their children sick out of a need for attention and admiration for themselves. But the reason FDIA can be quite difficult to identify is because the hyper-invested mother of a child with a fabricated illness looks a lot like the anguished mother of a child whose mysterious illness is still real.

I knew what was happening was true. My child had once been healthy, and now he was not. But I could also see the risks of pushing too hard. If it seemed like I cared *too* much, those in

First, Do No Harm

charge might stop believing me, leaving my child to become sicker still. As my late-night research sessions filled my hard drive, I knew if I couldn't stop looking for answers, I needed to keep more of that searching to myself.

One afternoon I picked up my son at school to take him in a taxi to his chorus practice near Columbus Circle. During that cab ride, he fell deeply asleep, and I couldn't wake him up when we arrived. I apologized to the very annoyed taxi driver and just barely managed to drag him, all unconscious sixty pounds of him, out of the cab and under the awning of a nearby building. I couldn't stomach him lying on the filthy sidewalk, so I sat down right there on Amsterdam Avenue, my back to the building, pulling him onto my lap, rubbing his back, trying to wake him up.

A passerby took in the sight of us, me sitting there on the ground, my child limply collapsed across me. Then he put his hand in his pocket and offered me a dollar.

It took me a moment to understand what he was doing.

"No, we're—not homeless," I said finally. Taking in his wide-eyed stare, I explained as best as I could. "There's just something really wrong with my kid."

The man was less fascinated than frightened. I could see through this stranger's eyes that what was happening was as out of control as it felt. I could also see I had an opportunity to prove it was happening. I asked the man to fish my phone out of my backpack and take a photo of us there on the sidewalk. Later, after my child woke up enough to get him home and into bed, I emailed the photo to every doctor I could think of, every single specialist who had ever seen my kid and may have sent us home wondering if I might have been making it all up.

Later that week I took my child for a full ultrasound and examination of his heart, as quickly ordered by the doctors who saw that photograph. When it was over and it was time for us to go home, my child lay unresponsive on the table. The cardiologist watched me attempt to wake him with ill-concealed alarm.

"This is it. This is why we're here," I said, still trying to shake him awake. "And now you're seeing it. This is what happens."

"Whatever is happening here, I don't believe there's a cardiac explanation," she said, backing away, her hands raised.

"Just say that it happened," I begged. "Just say that it's true."

In a six-page report, there it was, right at the end:

> *As a further note: I was quite struck by how unarousable the patient was after the examination. After he was finally able to be woken up, it was several minutes before he was alert enough to walk out of my office.*

Years later I remain grateful for those witnesses, these bits of information, that photo and those two sentences, proving that I was not complicating the matter with hypotheticals.

That it was indeed just as scary as it felt.

When my child and I first met with the pediatric sleep specialist, he immodestly introduced himself as "the very best in the world." He explained to me and my child's now-sizable team of doctors that this was almost certainly narcolepsy, that he'd never seen such a classic presentation, and he was only sorry he hadn't been consulted sooner. A sleep study would certainly prove him correct, and all that required was taking my child completely and immediately off all medication that might interfere with the readings. In my child's condition there wasn't any time to waste.

After the sleep study provided the proof we needed, the sleep specialist would prescribe narcolepsy medication, which would require waking my child in the middle of the night to administer it. Forever. I set aside my brief considerations of how future roommates and romantic interests might feel about such a task and told myself this could be the end of our searching. If we had an answer, even a difficult one, then we would know what should happen next.

After thirty-six hours with my child in a windowless basement, playing board games with him while he was monitored by myriad machines, encouraging daytime naps while I sat there in the dark, I met with the same sleep specialist and several other doctors to be given the results: no excessive sleepiness observed.

My child did not—could not—have narcolepsy.

"In my opinion, this child has been excessively medicated," the specialist declared, while staring firmly at me.

The other doctors demurred: while that had been considered, the dosages were much too small. Such a reaction would be completely paradoxical. There must be something else at play.

"I'm the greatest pediatric sleep expert in the world," the specialist said again, in case any of us had forgotten. He never took his eyes off me. "And if this isn't overmedication, then I don't know what it is."

The other doctors looked at the floor, unable to disagree with him, allowing to hang in the air the terrible possibility that he was right.

~~~

Six hundred years after Occam's razor, the Nobel-nominated medical researcher Theodore Woodward proposed a corollary: that when doctors heard hoofbeats, they should think of horses instead of zebras. The more common cause is the more likely diagnosis. The more common cause should be considered carefully before searching, at unreasonable cost to money and time and the patient's well-being, for causes that have a much lower probability.

An unexpected reaction to a medication, even if highly unusual, is still more likely than a patient having two different rare medical conditions. Something that the greatest sleep specialist in the world had never seen before could have only one explanation: the simplest one.

My child's passing out and cold sweats and lethargy slowly disappeared after the medications were discontinued. He never had another seizure. He outgrew the epilepsy by puberty, as had been predicted. Eventually it was like none of it had ever happened.

But he had still had multiple EEGs that showed something was wrong. But he had still lost consciousness at least twice before going on medicine in the first place. Those things had happened. Those things were also real. There would never be a single explanation, simple or otherwise, that would make all of it make sense.

Rereading my child's medical history a decade later, I am

reminded of the closest to a diagnosis that we ever got: "idiopathic loss of consciousness." I remember how excited I was to have gotten an official medical term for what was happening, at least until I got home and looked it up.

In modern medical speak, "idiopathic" means "we have no idea." It doesn't mean what has been observed is false or manufactured or imaginary, although sometimes of course that might be the physician's suspicion. But it also doesn't mean an answer. It means acceptance that there might never be an explanation. It means acceptance that you may never know for sure. Harder still is accepting that some of my child's suffering was certainly caused by medications my child should never have taken, prescribed to him by an overlapping group of medical professionals with the best of intentions, and rationed out to him every morning by a mother who thought she was taking good care of him.

The official term for that occurrence is "medication misadventure." In this case the person on that adventure was a small child, and that adventure included dozens of tests and doctors' visits serving mostly to tell him that there was something terribly wrong with him, and that no one was sure what it was.

My child is safe now, years beyond those hard times. While I can never know for sure, he may have been safe even then. I heard hoofbeats, and at first I really did think *horse*. Then I set that assumption aside, because I wanted so desperately for my child to be well, and believed that others knew far better than I did how to get him there. All these years later I still feel the shame of having led him ever further away from a feeling of safety, ever toward the message that he must be very sick indeed.

Maybe I did what any mother would have. Or maybe a different mother would have figured her kid just fainted sometimes, accepted that small and daily uncertainty. Maybe a different mother would have never embarked on such a misadventure in the first place, done all that searching, which could never have told me what I needed to know most: that my child was going to be okay.

I tell myself knowing things for sure isn't the only way to keep the ones I love safe.

I tell myself getting answers is not the same as getting well.

I try to forgive myself for the mistakes I made caring for someone I loved, someone my love was supposed to protect. The greater our love, the greater that terrible responsibility becomes: that we, first, do no harm.

Make New Friends, but Keep the Old

My rambling childhood home was once a doctor's office downstairs with living quarters upstairs, which meant there was a door at the top of the front staircase to a whole other part of our house: my grandmother's apartment.

My father's mother, widowed since her forties, had lived in our home for as long as we had. Her door at the top of the stairs was always open, although when I look back, while I would show up in my grandmother's parlor pretty much whenever I felt like it—joining her on the sofa, up past my bedtime, to watch *Knots Landing* while sharing the heating pad she kept across her lap—Gram pretty much came downstairs only to "visit" our part of the house on birthdays and holidays. (But not Easter, since on that day she'd serve us all ham and mashed rutabagas in her own dining room.) Due to her crippling arthritis, any trip down the stairs had to really be worth it. After she retired from working at her brother's insurance office, my grandmother descended only to go to church, out to dinner with her sister, or to attend monthly meetings of the Echo Club.

HAPPY TO HELP

The Echo Club was a group of eight ladies, including that same sister, whom my grandmother had known for most of her life. Every second Tuesday, they'd get together for lunch and an afternoon of pinochle and conversation. My late grandfather had given the club its name. Since all the women in the club talked at the same time, he is reported to have said, eavesdropping on their conversations for more than a minute meant you'd probably hear a repeat of something someone else had just said a few seconds earlier.

This was certainly my own experience of the Echo Club. Whenever it was my grandmother's turn to host, my mother would prompt me to make an appearance in Gram's card-table-stuffed parlor as soon as I got home from school. "Oh, here's Amy," Peg would say. "What grade are you in now, sweetheart?" Ten seconds later Stacia would say, "Oh, look. Amy's here." (Peg and Stacia were sisters, unmarried and inseparable.) Then twenty seconds later, Helen would look up from her cards and say, "Who's this, now? This *can't* be Amy."

I would obligingly accept the Echo Club's rolling good wishes and comments on how grown up I had become, and if I was lucky, I'd get a slice of Bundt cake for my trouble.

I had a similar ladies' club in my own life at that time—my school lunch table, where I sat with the same four girls, in the same seating arrangement, that had persisted for the last several years, the ironclad and unspoken rules of the middle school cafeteria having long dictated that seats and tables are permanent once chosen. Our table—Deanna, Nicole, Tina, Valerie, and me—featured the second-most-popular group of girls in our grade, the smart-but-nice girls, the "A" students who were at least still cheerleaders. If this was my caste, I was at peace.

Make New Friends, but Keep the Old

Then one day, as the seventh grade scrambled pell-mell down the stairs at lunchtime, one of the first-most-popular girls tapped me on the shoulder.

"You can sit with us if you want," Cathy said.

The invitation thrilled and frightened me in equal measure. I had no idea what I had done to merit such an opportunity. Also, one didn't simply sit elsewhere *once in a while*. If I sat next to Cathy once, I would be switching lunch tables permanently.

It felt like an unthinkable betrayal to the friends I would leave behind. And yet, if I moved to Cathy and Tammy's table, it meant walking right up to the boys who hung out on the edge of the parking lot at recess. It meant getting invited to an entirely different sort of sleepover.

Cathy stood there, awaiting my answer.

"Okay, thanks," I said, then slunk to my usual table, my peanut butter and jelly sandwich turning to the bitterest gall in my mouth as my usual tablemates, oblivious to what had just occurred, blathered on about the Smurfs.

It was suddenly clear to me just how uncool my friends were. They had no idea what I had just forsaken! Belatedly, I considered whether there was a chance they might have joined me. Was there a utopia in which we might link lunch tables and all be popular together? Could I, with the raw potential I newly understood myself to possess, sufficiently prepare any of these girls to become more popular alongside me?

As I looked around the table, I took stock of the group and decided that three of my friends—Tina, Deanna, and Nicole—showed possibility. But Valerie had to go.

The rules of middle school extended far beyond the cafeteria, of course. Among my peers it was just as immutable an expectation that we girls wear knee socks—and only knee socks—to accompany our plaid uniform skirts. Tights were unacceptable, and leggings didn't exist yet. When my mother insisted that I wear the perfectly nice green stretch pants that she'd ordered from the uniform company for my four-block walk to school, I would leave the house, take the pants off in our driveway, and shove them into my book bag, no matter how frigid a day it was. The risk of catching pneumonia was far less present in my mind than the idea of what would happen if Tammy or Cathy spotted me walking to school with pants on.

But Valerie, founding member of my cafeteria table group, was wearing sensible forest-green double-knit flares under her uniform skirt that very day. In the *cafeteria*, no less. She hadn't even had the good sense to take them off in the girls' lavatory upon arrival. She had no consideration for how badly this reflected on the rest of us!

Far worse was Valerie's recent lunchtime declaration that her life's goal was to become a Catholic saint. In order to grow in true holiness, she explained, she was going to take a vow of silence, and break it only when called on in class.

Being the considerate friends that the second-most-popular girls in seventh grade usually are, Deanna and Nicole and Tina and I had expressed our misgivings about this plan to one another in evening phone conversations. No way she could keep it up, we decided; it would last a couple of days, tops. But Valerie had been at it for a couple of weeks now and showed no signs of letting up, sitting there at our lunch table beaming beatifically in her green polyester pants. What would happen if Valerie were to join us at Tammy and Cathy's lunch table, only to sit there in pious silence? Or, even worse, speak up after all, and explain to the most popular girls in school that when she grew up she wanted to become a *saint*? All of us, our whole group, would be permanently canceled just by association. For our own good—and for Valerie's own good as well, since this was simply no way for someone to go through life behaving—our lunch table had to teach her a lesson by casting her out.

It can be surprisingly difficult to tell if a person who has taken a vow of silence understands that she has been ostracized. Under my direction, the rest of us stopped speaking to or acknowledging Valerie at our lunch table, but she still sat there in her same seat—not speaking, but not leaving, either.

I instructed the group that we were going to continue to ice her out until she got the hint and moved to what I considered the third-most-popular table (at that point, let's face it, not really "popular" at all). But after a few more days of executing my plan, my friend Deanna asked to speak to me in the parking lot after school. Representing her own interests, plus those of Nicole and Tina, Deanna explained they all felt too awful to continue. Plus, if they did, couldn't one of them be next to be thrown overboard? (As someone whose school cardigans were unacceptably hand-knit by her mother, Deanna was probably right to be concerned.)

Without troops on the ground, I could see my strategy was useless. Valerie would stay at our lunch table. And so would I. A week in middle school equals an eternity; Valerie gave up her vow of silence soon after that, and I resumed walking home after school with her as if nothing had occurred. My lunch-table invitation from Cathy would never be repeated. It was a limited window of opportunity, now gone for good.

HAPPY TO HELP

Our lunch table split up permanently soon after that anyhow, as we graduated and headed to two different high schools. At Central High it was far cooler not to appear in the cafeteria at all. The most popular lunch table was at Pappa's Pizza, where a few alpha females sat two tables down from the cash register with a rotating cast of football players. My clique of four freshman girls—Nicole and Valerie from my junior high lunch table, plus our new friend, Melissa—alternated between Sal's Pizza (no line) and McDonald's, hustling back into the school building just as the first bell rang for fifth period.

I found a good groove, and by sophomore year I had a very nice boyfriend, the lead in the fall play, and a little extracurricular activity with the senior I was also kissing onstage. One day I unburdened myself to Melissa in hushed tones at Sal's Pizza, telling her I didn't know what to do. That night Melissa called my boyfriend and told him I was cheating on him. She explained this to me the next day, in a note she folded into a tight triangle and handed to me after chemistry lab, claiming that she'd had no choice: he had the right to know the truth.

Part of me understood this correction by a member of my social group to be fair and justified—I needed to be corrected, just like Valerie had. And now I had to set things right. After ending things with the senior and obtaining my boyfriend's forgiveness, I thought I had done so. But upon further review of the evidence, Melissa, Nicole, and Valerie concluded that I "thought I was great." As punishment for this crime, they stopped speaking to me entirely. The word spread quickly, and I was soon shunned by most of the girls in our grade. At a large public

Make New Friends, but Keep the Old

school like Central High, a lot of them barely knew who I was, but in matters like these, it was definitely easier to side with the majority.

I did everything I could think of to make up for my sins. First, I tried hangdog sorrow; if these girls saw how much I was suffering, perhaps they'd commute my sentence to time served. No such luck. As the months went by, I slipped into depression. At least, I considered darkly, I had been cured of thinking I was great.

I had nowhere to go at lunch. My boyfriend, sweet but confused by my continued devastation at being ostracized, had the other lunch period. I was friends with a few boys in my AP World History class, but my sitting with them at Sal's would have cramped their style, not to mention their topics of conversation. So I started eating lunch every day in my drama teacher's office, not more than a windowed closet, full of books and papers and a woman kind enough not to ask why I kept showing up.

Eventually even Mrs. Langan had enough and called the other girls into her tiny office for a confrontation, her demanding they stop this nonsense, as I cowered behind her in her swiveling desk chair, begging them to believe that I had not put her up to it.

They did not. Mrs. Langan's attempted intervention only cemented their anger and redoubled their efforts to punish me. I began fantasizing about confronting these girls in the locker room, drawing a crowd, punching Melissa right in the nose. It seemed possible this was all it would take to stop their bullying. But I was afraid of what would happen if I was wrong.

It was the firebreak of summer vacation that saved me. Mrs. Langan called my parents and suggested I apply for a summer drama program at Northwestern. We didn't have the money for that, but I organized a garage sale of my family's old strollers and broken appliances, and my parents figured out how to pay the rest. It was my first time leaving home. I sobbed out the whole story during Approaches to Acting to an assorted group of drama nerds from all over the United States, afterward receiving a cathartic group hug. By the time I returned to Central High for senior year I was focused mostly on getting out, and it turned out my newfound indifference to what these girls thought of me was all that had ever been required to douse the flames of their righteous fury. We coexisted until graduation, but never reconciled before going our separate ways.

It was only years later, thanks to a therapist's gentle line of questioning about my latent distrust of female friendship, that I realized that high-school Valerie—cocaptain of the pompom squad, blithe destroyer of my ego—had only done to me what I had done to her first, back in seventh grade. How could I have forgotten? Valerie's evolution from novitiate-in-training to homecoming queen finalist—a transformation more gradually achieved than *Grease*'s Sandy Dombrowski's, but no less complete—had happened while I was absorbed by my own hero's journey. I had completely blotted out my careless cruelty, that I had, in fact, bullied her first, since that didn't exactly fit my blameless narrative. But what I did to Valerie had probably loomed as large in her life as her actions had in my own.

Back then, though, my primary takeaway was that female friendships were cliquey and tricky. I kept my relationships with my college roommates conflict-free, knowing better than to share my secrets. We were focused on our grades and our futures, far too busy for who said what to whom. Yale's Greek life was anemic, and it was one of the things I liked best about it—that

Make New Friends, but Keep the Old

there was no expectation of participation in all that nonsense. Sorority sisters would undoubtedly turn on you in a minute. I was safer without such allegiances. I didn't need letters on my sweatshirt to make friends.

Once I became an adult, then a parent, I had more friends than I knew what to do with. I was busy all the time: planning the fundraiser with the ballet moms, selling raffle tickets with the basketball moms, chairing board meetings for our sixty-three-unit apartment building. I felt called to any gathering that required a signup sheet, where I found the drama-free female friendship I had been seeking. I kept it productive; I kept it polite; I kept it moving. Sure, there was lots of pleasant chatting by the coffee station, but we were really there for the auction. For the church. For the kids. For the cause. Sometimes there were even name tags, so we could skip the awkward get-to-know-yous and just start stuffing the envelopes.

Once a year, on the last day before my kids' holiday break began, I'd glue crepe-wool beards on the eighth graders for their school's Christmas pageant. It became as much of a holiday tradition for me as decorating our tree. The same handful of moms appeared each year. We would laugh about our insane three-days-till-Christmas lists while we worked our magic on Isaiah and Joseph and the Three Wise Men. My friend Ann—a mom I've known since our oldest kids were three, a woman whose easy connection with everyone she meets always gave me a safe place to tag along—walked around one year taking pictures of the moms at work. "We matter too," Ann said, laughing. "I mean, come on. The kids don't have to be in *every* picture."

After the angels got their final sprinkles of glitter and the show had begun, we'd always linger a bit, talking while we packed up our supplies, but mostly about how we had to hurry out right after the show. We really had to run, to finish the shopping, to pack the car, to head out for the holidays.

But it was fine; we'd see each other soon enough.

During the pandemic, loneliness researcher Dr. Marlee Bower discovered that many of the social relationships we take for granted had proven unable to survive the extended separation. The people she interviewed who had significant relationships to draw on were okay; they just took those friendships online. It was the connections that were based on hobbies or shared work interests that didn't make it. And when the pandemic forced a sudden rupture of such interactions—the sort of connections Bower calls "peripheral contact"—the people who had relied on such relationships were the ones who were left truly lonely. Their friendships hadn't had enough of a foundation to make it.

Being a woman with too much to do had always given me a feeling of belonging, even as I ignored the group texts because I was in the middle of something. Even as I let a call from an old friend go to voicemail because it wasn't a good time to catch up. It was never a good time to catch up.

Then the pandemic created a strange rupture in all those friendships. After a few months, if I didn't know how one of my old friends had managed the worst of it, the fact that I had no idea served as proof we were never that close in the first place. If I called one of those sent-to-voicemail friends back now, just to chat, would she wonder why on earth I was calling her? Would

I be able to remind her of the things that once connected us? Would she remember me at all?

One of the hardest small losses of the pandemic was missing out on two years as a welcome visitor to my children's grade school, a parent community I'd known for most of my kids' lives. Two years of chatting in the stands at volleyball games were lost. Two Christmas pageants gone. And just as the restrictions on gathering in person were ebbing, our youngest child graduated, meaning my participation in that community had permanently expired. When the calls went out that fall for fun-loving parents to volunteer, there was no longer a seat for me at that cafeteria table. I was no longer able to find the friendship of other women simply by showing up where my kids were. What kind of a loser would show up even after her reasons for belonging were gone?

The day before the following year's Christmas pageant—the first one that grade school had had in three years, the first one in eighteen years in which my family had not taken part—my friend Ann texted me. Her kid had just graduated too.

Any interest in going to the pageant with me tomorrow? she said. **We'll just stand in the back.**

You don't think it will be too weird? I wrote back. A little too soon, a little too eagerly. Ann lived six blocks away. I hadn't seen her in two months.

Maybe a little, she wrote. **But who cares. I think we get to be there.**

We stood in the back of the house in the dark, behind the current parents who deserved the seats. I cried because I loved being back in the building. I cried because I always cry at the Christmas pageant. I cried because we had missed so much time together and it was not coming back. I cried because I recognized only a handful of the kids, which meant I really didn't belong there any longer.

Ann and I chatted out on the street after the show with the handful of parents we still knew. (Or that Ann knew. Ann knew everyone.) She had to run right afterward because her oldest was about to get home from college. But we should definitely have lunch soon, we both said. Send me some dates. For sure, let's see more of each other in the new year.

But who has time to do that work, attempting to align the impossible calendars of women with ailing parents and kids who are complicated and careers to lean into? Seeing the women we once connected with at all—let alone creating friendships that might last the rest of our lives—feels at once essential and impossible.

I once thought the Echo Club was the sort of thing old ladies without enough to do did: preparing deviled eggs, dressing up for each other, playing extremely complicated card games to fill empty afternoons. But my grandmother and her friends held their female friendships at the very center of their lives. They met every month for fifty years, whether they were dating, or getting married, or rationing, or looking for work, or having children, or burying children, or burying husbands. Once a month they shared their tragedies, illnesses, and joys. Only those on the outside saw it as silly conversations and cake. My grandmother made it to Echo Club when she could barely walk. Only death would part her from those friends.

Make New Friends, but Keep the Old

To make myself feel better, I tell myself that having the same female friends for a lifetime was never a possibility for me. Who grows up, marries, lives, and dies in the same square mile anymore? But it's also true that I've seen female friendships as temporary by design. Stick with your lunch table until it becomes necessary to cast someone aside. If you should be the one cut off, you can always join a committee. Or several. Just be sure to log off once the work is done. If that nice woman told you she'd love to stay in touch, she probably didn't mean it.

I've kept myself in peripheral contact with the vulnerability of true female friendship because it was easier to presume rejection than to ask to be included and know for sure. It feels frightening to call the friends I don't see but still think of. It feels more frightening to consider what may happen if I do not.

What I wish for most is a chance to climb those front stairs of my childhood home one more time and walk into my grandmother's parlor, where I never had to wonder if I'd be welcome, or whether she'd make room for me to sit next to her on the sofa, so we could just talk for a while.

Sometimes You Just Have to Laugh

When I was a kid wondering what life as a wife and mother might contain, my primary source materials were the women's magazines my mother brought home from the supermarket. I was a voracious reader, happy to consume whatever was on our coffee table: *Woman's Day*, *Good Housekeeping*, *Better Homes & Gardens*, and especially *Ladies' Home Journal*, with its flagship end-page series "Can This Marriage Be Saved?"

Each installment of "Can This Marriage Be Saved?" featured a relationship on the rocks from the male and female points of view (marriage at that time being viewed through a strictly heteronormative lens) and then a rendering on whether the relationship was salvageable, provided by a counselor at the American Institute of Family Relations—and, more important, by myself as reader.

Could these marriages be saved? I considered the evidence in earnest. Sometimes the relationship issues would involve secret second families and squandered savings accounts and other betrayals that seemed pretty unforgivable, even to me, a gradeschooler. But they were usually more gray-area sorts of shortcomings—almost always on the man's part—and the wife's excessive expectations often became the focus. So what if her husband stayed out too late sometimes and checked out the legs on the other ladies at church on Sunday mornings? Was that *really* a transgression worth a broken home? If her husband had a wandering eye, the answer to whether her marriage could be saved was always "yes," as long as the wife was willing to do what it took to rekindle a love life that had clearly become ho-hum.

There were exceptions, of course, ones even the American Institute of Family Relations granted as justifiable for a wife to be mad about. But even then, one had to consider the effects on the children. Divorce was presented as a last resort, failed marriage the worst-case scenario, and the best preventative was a perspective shift. *This might not bother you so much, Harried in Hoboken, if you just didn't* let *it bother you.* The cure-all was a helpful suggestion: lighten up a little.

What Harried in Hoboken was never told to consider was what she should do if she tried to laugh it off, but couldn't, because she was still angry. Or what the effect on her own happiness might be if she stayed.

But if Harried in Hoboken was supposed to lower her expectations for what wedded bliss should contain, that same slack did not extend to what her home should look like. With our big ramshackle house and all of us underfoot, my mother was no neat freak, but our home was clean and tidy, and that meant her work was constant. Once a month or so I'd walk in from playing Barbies at Susie Krupski's house and be stopped short by my mother yelling frantically from the other end of the house, "Don't walk through the kitchen! I just waxed the floor!" I didn't understand—still don't—what that meant, exactly, or how long

I would be banished, or why that labor was required on behalf of our kitchen linoleum, just that it was something my mother would spend an entire afternoon doing, and then an entire evening keeping us away from, only to have to do it all over again soon enough.

Feeding our large family was another constant. My mother clipped coupons from all those women's magazines and let me categorize them in the recipe box she'd take to Giant Market each week for a full-cart shop, something she called "going for an order." My mother's organization and forethought meant she spent less on groceries than you might expect. But like most of my friends' mothers, she took little joy in meal planning or preparation. Women had to cook every day back then; there was no Boston Market or Trader Joe's frozen section, not even a measly rotisserie chicken from the deli counter. Okay, there was Hamburger Helper, but the "help" promised was for the ground beef. Dinnertime was not a place to find fulfillment or to try new things. It was a means to an end, something to be gotten over with and then cleaned up afterward so my mother could get my little sisters in the tub.

Sometimes my mom would leave the *I Hate to Cook Book* out on the kitchen counter, the cheap yellowed pages held open with a can of cream of mushroom soup to the spattered recipe for Saturday Chicken. I would drop my school bag right there on the floor to flip through it, always starting with the introduction. "Some women, it is said, like to cook," the book began. "This book is not for them." My mother was among the unsung many who did not like to cook, which meant the *I Hate to Cook Book*, which combined passable recipes with a gimlet eye for the entire culinary enterprise, was a resource she kept close at hand.

The author, Peg Bracken, was an ad copywriter and mom of several. Her male editors told her that the book would never work, because all housewives—at least in their own estimation—considered cooking to be of sacred importance. A female editor was more able to see the book's extreme potential appeal, and the *I Hate to Cook Book* went on to sell many millions of copies. By the time I was reading it after school, Bracken's book had already been around for decades, but I still found it delightfully naughty and transgressive, as least as compared to the women's magazines from the supermarket. If I was also going to grow up to hate to cook, there would at least be opportunities to slack off. Bracken's book included recipes like "Stayabed Stew," where the person in bed mid-afternoon is the housewife herself—not because she's sick, but because she feels like it.

But Bracken was probably going more for comedic effect than for practical applicability. I remember laughing at the recipe for "Skid Row Stroganoff," but I don't remember my mother ever preparing it. And when I try to recall my own mother with a "Stayabed Stew" moment, allowing herself the luxury of putting her feet up, I can recall only a single time I walked in from school to see her lying on our den couch, eyelids fluttering. She was about thirty-five then, pregnant with her fifth child; her fourth child, still an infant, was presumably down for a nap. "I'm all right," my mother told me, half awake, responding to my confusion. "I just . . . need to lie here a moment." When my father got home from his accounting firm that evening at six-thirty p.m., dinner was served, as usual.

A career was no excuse for escaping wifely duties. Even women who worked outside the home as fabulously successful authors still owned the Sisyphean chore of deciding what was for dinner that evening. "There you are again at a quarter to six," Bracken wrote, "with your hat still on, staring at a pound of hamburger or a can of tuna." And sometimes with the doorbell about to ring at any minute, since it was assumed you'd be entertaining at home quite frequently. The *I Hate to Cook Book* listed chapters for canapés, girls' luncheons, children's birthdays, dinner parties, and your husband's boss coming over for dinner. Bracken's own boss apparently never came for dinner, but if he did, what to serve would still have been hers to sort out.

Still, the *I Hate to Cook Book* gave my mother reassurance that she wasn't a bad person because she found no joy in meal preparation. There was at least one other woman out there who was as tired of it all as she was; no attitude adjustment or perspective shift was required. Bracken called it a "hands-across-the-pantry feeling coming right through the ink. It is always nice to know you are not alone." But the lighthearted acknowledgment of that fact stopped there, the humor in the situation its point and its end. My own used copy of *I Hate to Cook Book* contains a written message inside underlining that this gift was, of course, just for laughs. *I know you like to cook,* the inscription says. *But it's fun to read anyway. Love from Rog and Jean.* The attractive penmanship suggests it was Jean who had done the writing and the gifting, while Rog, a silent partner in this enterprise, received half of the credit without ever knowing it had occurred.

What the *I Hate to Cook Book* never suggested was that women could either refuse to cook every single day or ask their spouses to participate. Bracken's sequel, *I Hate to Keep House,* was heavier on the concrete housekeeping advice, and more explicit about who would be absent from the conversation. "Husbands needn't concern us too much," Bracken wrote. "Husbands, with few exceptions, do what they want to do and what they think they ought to do, in fairly equal amounts, and they are not easily changed." In the book's 185 pages of advice for dusting the woodwork and defrosting the freezer, it is the only time the word "husband" appears. Bracken includes a list of household chores that a teenage boy might do (and, naturally, a much longer list for a teenage girl), but no lists for the men to whom her readers were married. Bracken's way to help a woman who had too much to do was to crack wise about a cleaning wonder called sel salt, available upon request at the grocer's for just fifteen cents; it was not to advise her that her workload was unfair, even impossible, and that her partner should be doing more.

But sel salt doesn't scrub the stains by itself. And the bandwagon fallacy that men won't help—therefore it's of no use to ask them—seems, at least from our modern vantage point, suspiciously convenient for about fifty percent of the population. But women like my mother readily accepted Bracken's central thesis, neatly summed up on the back cover of the *I Hate to Cook Book*: they could either laugh while cooking or cook while laughing.

Erma Bombeck proposed a similar approach to domestic drudgery in her weekly newspaper column "At Wit's End." Bombeck wrote fifteen bestselling books, but it was her column, in nine hundred newspapers for more than twenty years, that enabled a yearslong relationship with her devoted female readers. My mother's shoulders would shake with suppressed laughter whenever she read Erma's latest, and sometimes she would Scotch-tape a particularly pertinent Bombeck column to our avocado-colored refrigerator, like Martin Luther's missive nailed to the church doors. Poring over these columns, I'd hunt for what my mother thought was so funny, or at least so relevant to her own situation. Sometimes I got it; sometimes the jokes about Supp-Hose support stockings went way over my head.

But I don't think my mother put those columns there so the rest of her family would read them. I think she posted them for herself, so she could remember what Erma had said and laugh again at how true it was. And there was no better location than the refrigerator, since my mother spent more time in the kitchen than the rest of our family put together.

When Erma Bombeck started appearing on *Good Morning America,* my mother would shush us so she could listen to the small TV on our kitchen counter in the mornings while she made our school lunches. Everything Bombeck said suggested a life a lot like my mother's: sure, Erma may have gotten to pal around with Phyllis Diller, but she would still be taking her kid to Little League practice later. Bombeck was just one of the girls, someone who remained resolutely apolitical in her columns even as she became an ardent supporter of the Equal Rights Amendment (ERA). Despite having had an early groundswell of support, the ERA had become a deeply polarizing issue, stalling a few states short of the thirty-eight it needed for it to become law. Bombeck traveled to each of those states to speak out in support of the ERA's passage. Some bookstore owners removed Bombeck's books in protest. Conservative newspapers dropped her column, at least temporarily. Bombeck thought the rightness of her quest should have been clear. "Equality of rights under the law," she quipped, "may be the most misunderstood words since 'one size fits all.'"

My own state of Pennsylvania had been among the first to ratify the ERA, although we never discussed that in our grade-school history classes in Scranton. All I knew was that a lot of grown-ups seemed mad that the ERA existed, which confused me. How could anyone disagree that women were just as good as men? I finally asked my mother why a law that said men and women should be treated equally seemed so controversial. My mother thought about it, then sighed. "I don't know," she said. "I guess people think it's kind of silly. We don't need to have a law. We're equal already."

There was no point in a law (which never passed). There was no point in asking husbands to cook sometimes. There was no point in being angry or demanding that things be different. Sure, women could gripe a bit, that was allowed, as long as they did it with a sense of humor. Otherwise it was just whining, and whining was annoying, at least to the people who had to listen to it.

Just like I can remember seeing my mother with her feet up only once, I remember seeing her cry only once. One afternoon I walked into our kitchen, across the probably just-waxed linoleum floor, to find my mother at the kitchen table, her face in her hands.

"What's wrong?" I asked her, completely baffled.

"I can't do it anymore," she said, between heaving sobs, still covering her face. "I can't."

She had five of us then, including two under two. My father was at the office and would probably be working late. It was one of his "tax seasons" as a CPA, which had grown, along with his responsibilities, from two weeks in April to what felt like half of each year.

I just stood there watching my mother cry. What was there for me to say? What help could I offer? I didn't even know how to turn on the oven. But I did understand something for the first time. I saw my mother, just for that moment, as someone who might not always be as cheerful and steady as she seemed.

Someone who might not always love doing all the things she did for us.

Someone who might not want to do those things anymore.

I didn't know what to do with those feelings, so I avoided eye contact until she got up from the table.

Then everything stayed pretty much the same after that.

It was just like the "big sister poem" said, the one my mother had given me: she loved, and she laughed, and she got things done. Of course my mother liked to cook. That book about hating it? That wasn't really my mom. That was just for fun.

Or perhaps the Erma Bombeck columns taped to the refrigerator were secret messages to me, and that poem a mother's gift: the knowledge that I was not alone, the feeling of being understood, of existing together at wit's end.

Keep the Faith

In my household I'm told that I'm "just better" at things than the other people who live here, things like wrapping presents, remembering passwords, and knowing whose clothes are whose when they come out of the dryer. These little tasks—the noticing, the remembering, the ordering, the tracking—are the sort of multitasking most women stuff into the crevices of our attention, adding LEGOs to the online Target cart for an upcoming birthday party present while smiling and nodding on our Microsoft Teams meeting like nothing else is happening. The reward women usually get for doing this sort of work is our loved ones' wistful admissions that we're just so good at it.

We're just *better at it* than they are, that's all.

That women are naturally better multitaskers has been generally accepted as scientific truth over the last few decades. A study in the late 1990s found there was more "white matter" connecting the two hemispheres of women's brains, which facilitates connections among the brain's processing centers. Some social scientists suggested this might make switching between different sorts of tasks less difficult for women. Within the larger Mars/Venus conversation of that time—there were two genders, complete opposites in every way—it seemed obvious. Our traditional ways of existing in the world had been fossilized in amber over millennia because that was just how men's and women's very different brains had always operated. Women could do ten things at once and men could not, because that's just how we were wired!

In 2013, other scientists studied whether these assumptions around male versus female multitasking could be empirically proven. Their experiments sought to measure whether men's and women's levels of executive function—the ability both to plan tasks and to juggle multiple things at once—differed. In one experiment, male and female participants were given eight minutes to find a key in a field. At the halfway point, each searcher was interrupted by a phone call in which they were asked trivia questions.

The men and women did about the same on the trivia part; it was the key search where the two groups diverged. The female searchers tended to employ methods like starting in one corner and working back and forth across the field, lawnmower-style. The men tended to walk to somewhere in the middle of the field and then start looking, some of them wandering without any pattern to their searches at all. Guess which group was more successful in finding the keys?

The results of these experiments indicated that women did indeed outperform men in several multitasking paradigms. While the authors of the study warned that readers "should caution against making strong generalizations," the newspaper headlines and morning news shows blew past that hesitation, trumpeting once again the incontrovertible truth that women's biological, brain-based advantages make them superior at organizing, prioritizing, and keeping calm under pressure. What no one stopped to consider as an influencing factor for the noticing, the remembering, the ordering, and the tracking was whether the female participants in the study weren't better at these things simply because they'd had so much more practice finding things other people had lost.

The problem is that once we as women accept that we are "just better" at doing these small things, we tend to keep doing them; and in order to also keep doing the big things, we have no choice but to multitask. I write best with silence, a blank screen, notifications off, and nothing else to fracture my attention. And yet while writing this very page I paused to renew our vehicle registration, having just remembered spotting the expiration date on the sticker last night, and then to buy printer ink, which I remembered after going to print said registration. Neither of these things was drop-everything urgent, but whenever I resolve to clear my mind of all extraneous thoughts, the blank page in front of me becomes a field full of shiny, lost keys beckoning me to attend to them immediately.

In 2016 a broader study of multitasking—this time conducted by three female scientists—found "no significant gender differences in any of these measures of dual-task performance." In other words, men and women are equally bad at doing more than one thing at a time. Still, the biological superiority of women's multitasking persists as a stereotype. I hadn't read any of these studies until researching this chapter. I had presumed it was settled science that women's brains were wired differently.

So, it seemed, had the rest of my family.

As we cleaned up after dinner one night and our kitchen counter piled up with an assortment of drying pots and pans, I asked, with dishpan hands, if someone else might put them away where they belong.

"You're the only one who knows where they go," my oldest child said.

"They go where the pots and pans go," I said, "which is the cabinet right next to the stove."

"But which one goes *where*?" my husband said, like it was a tangram puzzle well beyond a nonprofessional's capacity, instead of an open space into which I would shove everything until it fit.

In reality, no one, irrespective of biology or gender, is very good at toggling among multiple assignments. The tax that multitasking levies on our mental processes and productivity is the same. Women aren't "just better" at finding lost keys while also answering irritating phone calls. But the assumption that we are means that women are often expected to multitask where men are not, doing six things simultaneously for each of our working hours rather than a still-difficult one or two. The myth that women possess some unique, nontransferable ability to anticipate and complete tasks was a fallacy in which I had wholeheartedly participated. I had been doing more work all this time *without* being any better at it. And now I also had a book to write, which would require as much uninterrupted attention as I could give it. For the next eighteen months or so, some of the extra work I did would have to be either set aside or redistributed.

I explained all of this to my family at the dinner table the following evening.

"Are you going to give us a list?" my husband asked.

"No. There's not an actual list or anything," I said. "I just mean, like, if you go to feed the dog and there's no food . . . go get her some food."

"I don't know what kind of food to get her." My seventeen-year-old was already opting out. "You get her, like, three different kinds."

"Because I just get her whatever looks good! It's not complicated, I swear."

"We don't know which pet store you go to," my daughter said.

"Any of them work," I said, there being three pet stores in a four-block radius of our apartment.

"I think you need to make a list," my husband said, "because you're better at noticing stuff. I'm happy to help, if you make a list."

"I don't *want* to make a list. A list would be work too. I'm just saying I need everyone else to do a little more around the edges. Like, put your water glass in the dishwasher . . . and if you notice the dishwasher is full, put some soap in and turn it on."

"But then when I go to turn it on, it won't," my husband said. "You're the only one around here who can get the dishwasher to work." He was right there—our dishwasher is a hothouse flower, rather fussy about its requirements, and the only one who has proven herself to have the magical, dexterous ability to turn it off, turn it back on, and then press "start" three times is me.

Was my family correct? Were there reasonable explanations for why I was the only one who could do the various tasks I wanted to hand over? And had I had an unwitting hand in creating those realities?

I asked my podcast co-host, Margaret, about this. She wondered whether there might be a household history of Mom wanting things a certain way. "Be honest," she said. "Would you secretly be a little mad if they put the pots and pans away and they weren't in the right places?"

I could see why my friend might have assumed that I, ever the Shirley to her Laverne, was the type of person who cares how pot lids are stacked. But while my inner compass might point toward the well organized, when it comes to dog food and shoes in the hallway, my standards were lower than my family was claiming they were. My maternal gatekeeping was not the problem. Our pantry's spices didn't have to be in alphabetical order. I just didn't want to be the only person who knew where the spices were.

Perhaps I needed to make myself more clear.

"I have to clear my mental decks to get the writing done," I told my husband over coffee that weekend. "And so I will probably need you to pick up the slack on some things. Or else those things can wait. Or get done at the last minute. Or just not get done at all. And maybe that's fine! I mean, it's all going to be okay!" I was apologizing my way out of my own explanation.

"All right. Let's start with the bills," my husband said.

"The bills are fine. We have a system." Well, I had a system. We'd decided as a couple years earlier, based on his frantic work schedule and my presumed female-brain penchant for organization, that I'd handle the bill-paying.

"We need a real system."

"We *have* a real system." All our bills were automated. I wrote six checks a year. It was the smoothest-running part of our household. It had also become, I suddenly understood, basically invisible to everyone who was not me.

Keep the Faith

"We're going to need a *better* system," my husband said, pressing the issue, probably imagining our electricity being shut off within the week. "You just said you're going to be really busy."

"Okay, yes. I did just say that. But I spend, like, an hour a month on our bills! They are not my time problem. I'm talking about everything else."

"You asked me where you could find more time," my husband responded, at the end of his usually considerable patience. "And I'm saying here's something you can outsource. And then you immediately say, 'But not that.'"

I couldn't really argue with that, so I dropped the line of discussion. The bill-paying continued as it previously had, and so did the "everything else" I had been hoping to address.

So did my frustration.

Why was my partner telling me to do what I did differently, when what I was asking for was the freedom to do less? Why were the things I was trying to hand over being hot-potatoed right back to me?

And did it mean there was no use in trying to change?

My other job—creating and producing a parenting podcast three times a week—also continued apace. Finding time to research the episodes was becoming tricky as well, although the show's constant near-term deadlines were always there, offering a comforting yet still productive alternative to writing, one far easier to accomplish than staring at a blank computer screen and willing the muses to visit me.

A podcast listener had sent in a question about how to deal with her four-year-old's increasingly difficult behavior. Whenever this mother tried to put new or different consequences in place, her child would have an epic tantrum, an even worse version of the behavior this parent was trying to prevent. *I've tried everything,* this mother said. *I am out of ideas.* So was I, but the resulting research led me to the concept of "extinction bursts."

Human beings reinforce one another's behaviors both positively and negatively, both intentionally and accidentally. Through our words and actions we reward the things others do that please us, thereby reinforcing those behaviors. Someone who is thanked for taking out the garbage is more likely to do it again. We can also offer negative consequences in order to disincentivize behaviors we do not appreciate; a child who is reprimanded for pulling the cat's tail will eventually learn to stop. Of course, this means our own behaviors are also continuously influenced by how others respond, and over time, our behaviors become conditioned toward those responses. In order to get what we want, we behave in ways that have historically elicited the responses we desire.

An "extinction burst" occurs when that learned pairing either disappears suddenly or is replaced by a different stimulus. Rather than simply stopping the previously conditioned behavior in its tracks, there will often be a sudden, dramatic, and negative behavioral response.

Consider what happens when someone puts money in a vending machine and pushes the button for their preferred snack. They have been conditioned to expect the chosen snack to fall into the delivery tray for easy retrieval. But what if, one day, that doesn't happen? What if the machine does not deliver the snack—and doesn't return the change, either? Does that person shrug and walk away, figuring they'll try for those Chili Cheese Bugles again tomorrow? More likely they'll push the buttons one to fourteen more times, try to shake the chips loose, and perhaps give the machine a righteous, useless kick before finally slinking off hangry.

Keep the Faith

This is an extinction burst at work. When a conditioned behavior is met with a new, surprising, and unwelcome stimulus, a negative behavioral response will occur—usually with increasing volume and frustration—at least until it becomes clear that resistance is futile. Even the most ill-tempered among us will eventually come to accept that the vending machine is not going to change its mind.

Here is what is most essential to know about extinction bursts: behavioral psychologists agree they do not last forever. These eruptions will lessen, eventually stopping completely, as long as the previous and expected stimulus is not put back in place before then.

But most parents of tantruming toddlers have never heard of extinction bursts, and most parents lack the apathy of a vending machine. When faced with an apoplectic child drawing stares in the aisles of Target, parents often reverse course, give in to the tantrum, and buy the desired candy or toy—regaining equilibrium for that moment, but also reinforcing for their child that screaming is a great way to get what they want. In the future, if they don't get what they want, they need only scream louder and longer, until their parent gives up.

What most of us fail to understand is that the extinction burst is not a sign that a new boundary is not working—it's the first signal that it is. It only feels like failure in the moment; all we need to do is weather the storm. But that moment is when most of us give up.

However, if we are ready for extinction bursts, if we know they are likely to occur, we will know what to do next, which is—as I would go on to tell the mother of the tantruming toddler in that podcast episode—to stay the course. Do not turn back. I told that mother she should welcome and withstand the extinction burst, because it is what was going to happen in the moments just before true change.

My children are years past toddlerhood. My spouse is a good bit older than that, as am I. But when I tried to change our conditioned family procedures, they responded by pleading ignorance, then their inability to change. Then doing it louder. But they weren't being intentionally unsupportive, I realized. They were just being human. They were all for my being more creatively fulfilled, but not so much the them-becoming-busier part. And why should they have been? It was better for them the other way. Why should they want to take on thankless responsibilities I had conditioned them to believe never had to be theirs? Of course the first and second things they did were to hit everything back across the net to me.

But that resistance might have been temporary were it not for what I did next. When I took back all the little things I had attempted to hand over, all I did was further cement that expectation for every one of us. Including myself. Changing that narrative meant changing it in my own head first. What if it wasn't easier if I just did it myself? What if I wasn't "just better" at turning on the fussy dishwasher and knowing how much longer to cook the chicken? What if I didn't have the proverbial eyes in the back of my head, or an inborn ability to remember all the things?

What if it turned out that I wasn't better at anything at all?

What if I asked for help, and then I got it?

It's easier for me to accept assistance when it feels like it's in service of the public good. The help should ideally make things better for everyone, not just me. During the obvious parts of my three pregnancies, whenever someone offered me a seat on the subway, I'd take it every time, even if I was fine, even if I was getting off at the next stop. I wanted to reinforce it as a habit that should be repeated for the next pregnant person. I would condition that behavior by offering a positive response: "Why, yes, I would like a seat! Thank you so much." Okay, yes, the sitting down part was nice also. But I was doing it for the good of the next pregnant person, for my baby, for *the whole world*—not just for my own more comfortable ride to 72nd Street.

Increasing the demands on the people I lived with, asking for more of their participation in our family systems, felt selfish. I was requesting a sea change from the people closest to me; they feared that change, and so did I, resisting the very realignment I was seeking. As psychologist Darcy Lockman has explained, "Our culture's particular emphasis on feminine family devotion leaves women more vulnerable to guilt and then despair when they find themselves with outsize nonfamilial obligations." This book was an obligation both outsized and nonfamilial. I needed to ask more of the people I loved to get it done. Things would indeed get a little less convenient when I was less available. But when I requested that everyone else start doing more, and was not immediately hoisted aboard a puffy cloud of affirmations and loving support, I had a resistance burst of my own. *Thanks for nothing. I'll just rage-clean the apartment myself, I guess.* I knew *this wouldn't work.*

But that someone expresses displeasure with a boundary doesn't mean that boundary is doomed or mistaken. My discomfort with creating such a boundary was another sign not to reverse course, that something might have been just about to change.

Maybe something new would be created: A pause. A reconsideration. Maybe something else was just about to happen.

Six months after the Dinner Table Conversation of Resistance, I was sitting at that same table one afternoon, eight tabs open on my laptop, clicking furiously. My husband walked by between Zoom calls.

"We're out of dog food."

"Oh God, are we?" I said, not looking up. "Okay. I'm on hold with the bank about that missing deposit. Then I need to get this package downstairs before UPS shows up. Then I have a call. Then I'll go get it."

My husband left the room.

Twenty minutes later he texted me: **I can't find the food she likes. Which aisle is it?**

My spouse had gone to the pet store. I hadn't noticed that the dog needed food; he had. Even then, I still assumed it was mine to deal with when he brought it up, since it had always been before. But my partner had taken care of it. He had just gone, without explaining why he couldn't.

Without huffing, "Fine! I also have a call, but whatever. I'll go."

Without saying, "No problem, honey. I'm happy to help," because it wouldn't have been "helping" me—it would have been helping the dog. As I would probably have uncharitably reminded him.

I was multitasking as much as I ever had, sitting at our kitchen table, where writing a book has been proven never to occur. But change had still occurred while I wasn't looking.

Keep the Faith

I can't find the food she likes. Which aisle is it?

Extinction bursts might accompany that change, but now I knew to expect them.

They're just what humans do. Change is what happens next.

It's all the way in the back, all the way on the right, I responded.

Two minutes later my husband texted me a photo. Some kind of dog food I'd never seen before. Liver with cheese. Definitely not what I would have picked.

Not that one, I started to type. **Look at the top shelf. Find the ones with the orange stripe.**

I backspaced, started again.

I bet she'll really like that, I answered.

And she did.

We're All in This Together

My husband used to have a job with the title of chief risk officer. Most large corporations have one, particularly since 2012, when a single trader known as "the London Whale" lost more than six billion dollars for JPMorgan Chase right under the noses of everyone else who worked there. No one had predicted one of the world's largest banks could suffer such losses due to one of its own employees. But in retrospect, it seemed that someone *should* have.

Chief risk officers monitor both the workings of their own firms and the events of the larger world for potential threats. It can be a disconcertingly large and vague assignment: make sure nothing bad happens to your company, because if something does, it will be your fault for not having foreseen it—even if what happened was completely unpredictable right up until the moment it occurred. Chief risk officers scan the horizon for everything they know could go wrong, but the largest risks are often the Unknown Unknowns, the things even the best Watcher on the Wall could never have imagined. As my husband told me back when he had that job, every year that passed without anything bad happening felt like a year closer to a time when something eventually would. And that would be a time, inevitable and terrible, when one would really not want to be chief risk officer.

Not that I ever angled for that particular title myself. Why have two to a family? I may enjoy planning ahead, but I have never been one to borrow trouble. So I really wasn't that concerned when the news said that a hundred people in China had died of a new virus. Then one American on a cruise ship. We were always supposed to worry about something or other: avian flu, murder hornets, flesh-eating bacteria. Then the news would stop mentioning it, leaving it half remembered, something that had happened a world away.

My husband thought we should probably still stock up on some of the basics, bottled water and soup and paper towels, but as I cleared the shelves of our coat closet for these supplies, they seemed just as likely to remain forgotten and unused as the deflated basketballs and outgrown snow boots I was discarding. If it made my husband feel better, fine. Preparation was preventative. Didn't forecasts of rain always prove wrong on the days you brought an umbrella along? Having what you need for that predicted thunderstorm ensures the day will remain sunny and bright.

But here's the other thing about packing that umbrella: I'm the dum-dum who notices it really does look like rain outside, then dismisses that notion and leaves the umbrella at home because the Weath'R Pro app on my phone says it's going to be partly sunny. What am I going to believe, my own eyes?

We're All in This Together

Spring break was on its way, and the five of us were headed to Florida for a family friend's wedding. I set aside any unease about whether that was still a good idea. Any bit of darkening sky on the news would be quickly followed by a press conference explaining that there was really nothing to worry about, that we should be good citizens of New York City by conducting our business largely as usual.

The night before we were to leave, my husband waited until the kids were out of the room to tell me someone at work said he'd heard "they" were considering closing the bridges and tunnels.

After dinner we told our kids to pack all their schoolbooks in their bags. Just in case. What did we have to lose but a couple of extra-heavy suitcases? The next day we flew to Florida, wearing masks my husband's bridge-and-tunnel rumormonger friend had procured for us, with laptops and chargers and extra medications, but also with a curling iron, cuff links, and high heels for the wedding, because surely this all would turn out to be overblown; surely we were worrying about nothing; surely we would be fine.

Our phones blew up as soon as we landed with texts from our family and friends:

The wedding is canceled.
Everything is closed. Don't even come. We're so sorry.
A local state of emergency has been declared.
Did you see?? They just closed the schools for the rest of the month!!

This last text inspired a cheer from my kids in the back seat, until my oldest son's phone dinged with his personal version of This Just Got Real: the NBA had canceled the rest of their season.

The kids waited in the car while we maxed out a shopping cart at the closest supermarket we could find. Then we drove to the house, put the groceries away, and closed the door behind us. It was all real now. But we were safe. We had what we needed. We could definitely make it.

Even for two whole long weeks.

Five days later, I was driving to the grocery store. We were out of ice cream and pretzels. I figured I'd just run in. My daughter, also jittery with cabin fever, came with me for company. We drove with the windows down, but just because the air felt good. My daughter had had a weird stomach bug for a day or two, but she was fine now, almost too good, experiencing that bounce-back relief of feeling like herself again.

Inside the grocery store was different. There was an unease (yes, even in Florida). One-way arrows were taped to the aisle floors. Customers gave one another wide berth, obeying the new rules without any thought of resistance. I thanked the woman who checked us out for the essential work she was doing. She did not answer. I hurried back to the car, feeling the need to get home as soon as possible, to close the door and mean it this time.

On the drive home I suddenly felt so dizzy I had to pull off the road and stop the car. I had a pain in my abdomen I couldn't quite identify. Was this what a panic attack felt like? It wasn't that I was hyperventilating. I just felt sort of overcome.

We're All in This Together

Get a grip, I thought. *You're giving yourself an ulcer. There's no reason to be* that *worried.*

After a few minutes' rest on the steering wheel, my daughter saying, "You okay, Mom?" in a small voice, I managed to drive us home, then had to sit for a moment before bringing in the groceries. After I did that, I felt so worn out I had to lie down. The couch felt too far away; I lay on the floor.

I was still there an hour later when my sons came downstairs.

"What are you doing on the floor?" my younger son asked.

"I just need a minute. I feel really weird."

"What time is dinner?" my older son asked. Mom being sick was not something that could occur in my teenagers' worldview. It didn't compute. They didn't argue with it; they just stepped around it.

My husband walked in. "Where's Mom?"

"She's on the floor," my daughter announced.

My husband stood over me.

"I'm fine. I just feel weird," I said.

"Weird like how?"

"Like I can't move. I'm fine. I'll get up in a minute." I willed myself to stop being so dramatic. Even if this was an anxiety attack, I simply would not accept it.

I thought of Ma Ingalls from the *Little House* books I'd always adored. Ma didn't lie down on the floor when the locusts came, when snarling wolves paced right outside the door. I was part of a long line of pioneer mothers protecting their families, who remained ever cheerful and resourceful in the face of adversity. No matter what happened, Ma Ingalls moved ever forward, making the daily bread, pressing her palm gently into the top of each loaf as the only sweetening her family needed. The least I could do was get up off the floor and throw together some chicken enchiladas.

The news had said the symptoms we were supposed to be watching for were bad-cold sort of stuff. Cough and fever. Not stomach pain, and not a weirdly complete exhaustion, which was why I didn't connect my own illness with my daughter's stomach bug a few days earlier.

Two days later I woke up unable to take a deep breath. I waited until my sons were on their Zoom classes before I told my husband.

"You're fine," he said. "I mean, I'm sure you're fine. You're not coughing. And you don't feel hot. You're definitely fine."

He was right, of course. He was definitely right. Until I woke up the next morning unable to get out of bed.

My son texted at eleven thirty, waking me out of a deep sleep:
What's for lunch?
    Can't get out of bed. Make ramen?
Only have twenty minutes til next Zoom class!!

I remember wondering, as I drifted back into unconscious slumber, how I had managed to raise a near-adult who thought it would take more than twenty minutes to boil water.

The next morning it was my husband who couldn't get out of bed. "But this isn't the same thing you have," he said. "This is different. I feel *awful*."

Thus began the time-honored traditional partner dance, passed down through generations of married couples: I'm the One Who's Sick Around Here (Actually). It was man flu with terrifyingly high stakes, conducted in frantic whispers just out of earshot of our three seemingly perfectly healthy children.

But now that my husband was telling me how incredibly sick he felt, I felt justified in calling my doctor's office and scheduling a telehealth appointment. It was late; I could see she was still in the office.

"I mean, yes. It sounds like you might have it," she said.

At least I knew for sure what we were dealing with. I asked her what I should do next, since she would know.

"Don't leave the house. And *don't* go to the hospital. There's really nothing they can do. Don't go unless your lips are turning blue." She paused. "And, I mean . . . even then."

That was the moment when I, chief risk officer, realized it was too late: the thing I was supposed to be watching for had already occurred. I was sick. So was my husband. One or both of us might get sicker. And if we did, I had never heard a medical professional more honest about her inability to help.

The tightness I felt in my chest was not my imagination. It was happening. The wolf had gotten inside. And we were entirely on our own.

The next day my older son got a high fever, one that was easy to detect even without a thermometer because his cheeks looked like he'd been slapped. But after a day or two he felt fine. His fifteen-year-old brother never felt sick at all and joined him in fervent agreement that I, their father, and their younger sister—who had by then been knocked back down by the virus—were definitely *not* sick with coronavirus, absolutely not laid low with what the news by now said was putting robust fortysomethings on ventilators. I was too weak to mount a counterargument. At least they had figured out how to make their own soup.

We were now down to our last couple of cans of Campbell's, and I wasn't sure who was supposed to go get more, since my husband and I were both too contagious and sick to venture out, and none of our kids could drive. If there were other people around in the neighborhood, we'd seen no sign of them, and what would we say if we could? "Nice to meet you. We have the plague. We'd love it if you could stop by!"

I thought of Ma Ingalls again, blizzard outside, Pa trapped somewhere in it on his way back from town, the nearest neighbor across the river. How Laura played with darling Charlotte, her rag doll, all through that evening, believing their cabin to be cozy and warm.

The nights were the hardest part. I'd moved to the spare room, hoping I wouldn't give whatever I had to my husband. But even after he also got sick, sleeping alone meant fewer interruptions. So I kept crawling up the extra flight of stairs after self-assessing my chest-tightness levels in case they worsened overnight.

One night I woke up to see a woman staring at me from the corner of the room. She was wearing yoga pants and a zip-up sweatshirt. A purse over her shoulder like she was heading out to run errands.

"What are you doing here?" I said, my heart pounding.

She didn't answer.

"Hello?" I said again, sure this time I was hearing my own voice out loud.

She didn't respond.

I closed my eyes. I opened them again. She was still in the corner.

"I KNOW YOU AREN'T REALLY THERE," I said then, not really knowing that at all, but figuring an actual person would feel obliged to contradict me. Or at least move.

But the intruder, whoever she was, just stood there.

I didn't scream. Mostly because I didn't have the lung capacity. But I was pretty sure this person I was seeing was not actually there. On the other hand, she was probably not a ghost, seeing as she was dressed in athleisure. What phantom would rise from the dead dressed in Lululemon? She also wasn't transparent or fuzzy; she was there in full color, so real I felt like I could reach out and touch her, though there was no way I was going to try it.

The final bit of evidence I considered, still lying there under the covers, was that if she were a ghost, she didn't seem to have much of an agenda. Even the Ghost of Christmas Yet to Come took Scrooge places and pointed at stuff. This apparition was just standing there blinking at me, unsmiling, but with great reserves of patience.

And that's when I finally realized that I was hallucinating.

At first I was relieved. *See that, silly? It's not a ghost, you're just having visual delusions!* Then I considered whether this was really the preferred outcome. My virally infected brain, usually confined to the thoroughly practical, was throwing off all sorts of sparks. That meant I must be as sick as I had feared.

HAPPY TO HELP

But if true danger had come, in the guise of the Ghost of Coronavirus Uncertainty, she was just sort of hanging out at the foot of my bed. If I could just let her be there, without touching her or ordering her to leave, perhaps we could remain on friendly terms. She might eventually decide to leave on her own.

I slowly got better. So did my husband. It would take at least a month before I could go upstairs without pausing halfway, but each day I felt a little stronger. The further in our rearview mirror it became, the more my husband asserted that we hadn't been *that* sick, hadn't had Covid after all. Not even when, weeks after we realized we could no longer taste the coffee or smell the Mr. Clean, experts added "loss of taste and smell" to the lengthening list of mysterious symptoms. But I was certain it had all really happened, and that was very good news. Not only had our family survived, we were now guaranteed to be safe. No one could get Covid more than once! Scientists said so!

It was the end of April before I stopped to notice that my twelve-year-old daughter had not really gotten better. Not gotten better at all, which was very strange, because the news kept saying kids couldn't get sick from Covid.

"Gosh, she's still feeling draggy?" her doctor would say. "Well, give it a week."

Give it another week.

Then her doctor said it was time to get her out of bed, but my efforts to take her on slow walks around the neighborhood never got past the end of the driveway. We'd return to her room so she could stare dully at the wall while I read her a dystopian youngadult novel about teenagers surviving a grim postapocalyptic landscape. If art was imitating life, neither one of us acknowledged it.

After six weeks, she had become too weak for remote sixth grade, too dizzy to come downstairs for dinner, too exhausted to take a shower. I was so relieved she never took a sudden turn for the horrible that it took me a long time to understand that she was getting worse slowly.

"It feels like an elephant is sitting on my chest," she said.

I called the pediatrician again.

"It's strange," the doctor said. "She really should be better by now."

"She's worse. She's telling me it's harder and harder to breathe."

The doctor suggested I find a pulse oximeter somewhere. If we could measure the levels of oxygen in her blood, it could reassure us that despite what she was reporting, my child was in fact just fine. I called around, found one in a medical supply store an hour away, and drove back feeling much better. The oximeter was all we would need.

I called the doctor back over FaceTime once I was home. My daughter's pulse—lying in bed—was 140, which I knew was weirdly high. But her oxygen level was a 91. I figured we were on a standard grading scale here: 91 out of 100? Squint and that's an A-minus. I could stop worrying. My child was fine.

The doctor paused. "Make sure it's on her finger right," she said. "Let's try that again."

We tried again. It was.

I only understood later that what the pediatrician was probably considering, in the second pause that followed, was that an oxygen level of 91 was definitely not fine. That a level of 90 or below would have indicated the need to call an ambulance. "I think," she finally said, smiling cheerfully because my daughter was there next to me watching her on my laptop screen, "that you have waited long enough."

My daughter cried when I told her we were going to the hospital. Not because she was frightened of what that might mean, but because the hospital was twenty minutes away, and she felt too sick to take that long of a car ride. My hands shook as I packed a bag with the dystopian-teen book we'd been reading, and snacks, and our health insurance card. I added pajamas, in case we were staying, and made us face masks from bandannas and hair ties, something one of my kids had seen on TikTok.

I kept up a nervous chatter with her the whole way to the hospital, my adrenaline coursing out in prattling about nothing, the way I did when she was a toddler in the back seat and I wanted to prevent her from nodding off before I could get her home and into her crib.

We pulled into a hospital parking lot that was almost completely empty. Two people in hazmat suits and plastic face guards manned a card table under a makeshift tent, scrolling through their phones, clearly unused to customers. They handed us paper masks to replace our homemade TikTok ones, then ticked through a few questions on a clipboard.

Has the patient had a fever?

Has the patient had difficulty breathing?

When I said yes to those questions, they dug around for the thermometer and another clipboard, still without any particular urgency. Lots of people showed up convinced they had this thing. The news liked to get people all riled up for nothing.

Has the patient experienced loss of taste and/or smell?

Has anyone in your family recently traveled outside the United States?

Have you been in contact with anyone from New York City?
Yes. Yes. Yes.

With each answer we gave, I watched their eyes widen further, the only parts of them I could see. Then they rushed us into an exam room through a special entrance. A series of doctors asked my daughter lots of questions. They gave her two bags of IV fluids. They gave her a Covid test, which would take two weeks to come back negative (a full eight weeks after she'd been infected, useless in the extreme).

And then, when her pulse got down from 140 to 130 a few hours later, they told us we could go home.

My worst fears—my child in the ICU, me quarantining there with her—or even more terrifying, sent home without her—had not come to pass. But it was hard to take much comfort in leaving without any answers.

"Don't worry, Mom! She'll be okay. Kids don't really get sick from Covid," the nurse explained as she disconnected her IV.

"She's really sick right now," I said.

The nurse didn't answer. She was probably thinking I should be grateful my child didn't need a ventilator. That the hospital was discharging someone who was still just as ill as when she arrived was bad news only for the person taking her home.

I did not know how to make my daughter well, or how long it might take to get her there, because no one knew what was wrong. Her chest X-rays were clear, and her cardiac workup showed no organ damage. This was presented as proof she couldn't still be ill, despite her low oxygen, racing heart, and inability to complete thoughts. I alternated between letting her lie in bed all day and putting on a tough-mom persona, telling her we were getting out in the sunshine and that was that. But any activity I forced on her seemed to make her even weaker for days afterward.

It would not be until June, after my daughter had been in bed for months, that I would finally read an article explaining exactly what she had been experiencing: the long-term persistence of mysterious symptoms after an initially mild Covid infection. For this growing number of patients, even small amounts of exertion made their conditions much worse. Medical professionals were largely at a loss as to what was happening, but the commonality of these patients' symptoms was getting harder to ignore. I read the article over and over again. It was uncertainty upon uncertainty, but it was happening, and it was what was happening to my child.

There weren't supposed to be gray-area complications for Covid. Either you died or you'd be fine. To this day, many people still roll their eyes at the idea of long Covid, even though biochemical markers have been identified proving its existence and pathology. Others, including some medical professionals, are still telling us that it couldn't have happened to children. This is probably easier than accepting the uncertainty of all post-viral illness, its confusing presentations, its all-encompassing weirdness. My daughter had been taken over in the strangest of ways: tremors in her legs, buzzing sensations in her arms and hands, forgetting ordinary words for things she used all the time. It's more reassuring to psychologize such symptoms than to accept that what's happening is real, without sufficient explanation, and certainly without cure.

At least when it's not happening to someone you love.

We waited, and we waited, and we agreed to have more patience still. I tried to accept the lack of control I had over her recovery. Then someone would mention that quercetin was good for inflammation, and off I'd run to the health food store.

The last thing in the world anyone would have wanted to happen was the one thing that somehow helped. A year after my daughter first got Covid, she became infected with a new variant. (So much for not being able to get Covid more than once.) While I was terrified as she became sicker still, my child then recovered to a much greater state of health, as if fighting off the new infection had somehow cleared out the old one as well.

And in the months and years since, my daughter has slowly won back a fairly typical life, although she may never regain the stamina she had before she got sick. Others with long Covid have shown little to no improvement, and even those who believe the symptoms they report are still struggling to determine how to help them. For our family, Covid has become less something we survived than something we have learned to live with, accepting our lack of control over its constant presence in the corner. At first, I was afraid of it. Then I yelled at it to go away. I slowly learned to do what seems to work best for my child: to let it be, and try to spend more of each day forgetting that it is there.

―᠊᠊᠊᠊᠊᠊᠊᠊᠊᠊᠊᠊᠊ↄ

In the spring of 2022, when society had driven the sixth or so stake into the heart of the pandemic, when the trees were in bloom and vaccination appointments were plentiful, my daughter I and went out to dinner with a group of her school friends and their parents. Even the grown-ups were giddy to be at a restaurant, masks off, together again on the other side of two really hard years.

"I told my kids that is it! We're not even testing anymore," one of the parents declared after we toasted to putting the hard times behind us. "I told them I don't care what the school says! I don't care if you have a sore throat! I don't care. We are *so done* with Covid."

As the other parents mostly murmured their assent, how they too were fed up with Scrabble and sourdough starters, I locked eyes with another mother across the table. She had lost a parent to Covid. Her husband had too.

"Well. I mean. Getting Covid can be pretty bad," I protested to the table, but too quietly, so only the mother sitting across from me heard.

She looked at me but didn't say anything. She didn't have to.

The pandemic was supposed to be a universal experience, except it wasn't, not at all. Everyone I know had a pandemic that ranged from lousy to impossible, including that parent who was inconvenienced by all the testing. But in some houses what people survived was the homeschooling of three kids and the specter of life without toilet paper.

In some houses people died, or almost died, or never really got better.

And in some houses people strove mightily to hide how frightened they were, so that those under their care, those they loved the most, might at least think they were safe.

In some houses people remember the pandemic mostly for its silver linings. In houses like ours, the ones where it got inside and stood at the foot of the bed, we remember it as real and frightening and terrible. Being chief risk officer through such a time meant increasing my tolerance of uncertainty, understanding my lack of control over the dangers that might await in the dark, then standing sentinel in that very place.

The ones chief risk officers love most are drowsy in their beds, drifting off to dreamlands in which they're done with danger.

And I'm Ma Ingalls, by the door in her rocking chair, singing her kids to sleep with a shotgun on her lap.

No Hard Feelings

It's said that the toughest thing about acting is all the rejection, but that's not really true. Being repeatedly rejected to your face, being turned down and then told why you were found wanting, would certainly be difficult. But that's not how auditioning works. Here is how it actually goes: you get the appointment, you prepare your materials, you perform for some people behind a table, they say "thank you," and then you leave. Then, far more often than not, you never hear anything about that role again. Your phone will *not* ring. The silence is how you eventually accept that you did not get that job.

Sometimes the phone rings, and it's a callback for a recurring role on an HBO limited series playing the best friend of an Oscar-winning actress. Then there's another callback, and then they "pin" you, and ask you to verify that your passport is current, and tell you to hold the last two weeks in May, and *then* the phone doesn't ring.

The toughest thing about acting is all the ghosting.

After years of auditioning, it does get easier. You assume the call won't come. You clear how desperately you want to perform Shakespeare in Central Park from your consciousness before the elevator even gets back down to the lobby. You stop clocking the creative team's reactions while you're doing your scenes. You stop wondering why they picked someone else and not you.

And, okay, yes: once in a while, if it's an incredible opportunity, if you feel like you nailed it, if you've been waiting for the phone to ring despite knowing better, you can ask for feedback. Never directly—such requests go through your representatives to theirs, then eventually back to you, several business days later. That feedback never sounds like rejection. It also never sounds like the truth. *She did great,* they always say. *Please tell her we said so. The team just went in another direction.*

No matter what they say, a small part of you will still believe the only thing that keeps you going: that you weren't good enough, but if you do it all perfectly, absolutely right next time? You'll get the part.

Like most children, I believed that "astronaut" and "princess" and "Yankees pitcher" were reasonable and widely available career paths, and whenever anyone asked me what I wanted to be when I grew up I would say something just as glamorous and unlikely. I was not a showbiz kid being trucked to go-sees and agents' offices, because even if my mother hadn't had my younger brothers and sisters to take care of, New York City was a hundred miles away, and she was not the Mama Rose type. I had never been in a play or a commercial, had never taken an acting class. I was never the class clown, never the one in trouble for talking and goofing around too much; no one who knew me would have said, "This child is born to entertain." And yet I'd known I wanted to be on stage ever since I could remember having an ambition for my future. Certainly it was about the attention, the idea that I might be in the spotlight with everyone else watching. Being an actor would also give me explicit permission to hold the microphone. If people paid to sit there in the dark and see you in a role you had earned by being the best, then there could be no question when it was your turn to talk. Everyone had already consented to listen, in full, to what you had to say.

Career aims usually morph into something more reasonable as we get older. If no child dreams of being an insurance claims adjuster, it is at least a future with a discernible means of approach. But I remained fixated on becoming an actor, and my parents neither pushed me toward this cockamamie notion nor tried to dissuade me from it. Even if they had their misgivings, I probably did not seem like someone whose mind could be changed. If becoming an actor was about wanting it enough, I had that to spare.

As I got older my acting dreams became more specific. I envisioned a have-Hedda-Gabler-will-travel life after college, living out of a suitcase and playing leading-lady roles on theater stages everywhere, granting audiences the cathartic recognition of their own humanity. That I would become renowned for such performances was part of those daydreams, although my fantasies never drifted toward the Academy Awards or the Hollywood Walk of Fame. It would be shallow to dwell on such things. Los Angeles was also three thousand miles away. Acting didn't seem risky or crazy to me; moving across the country without a friend or a job definitely did.

On the other hand, Los Angeles was the fabled Land of

Opportunity for actors, the place where you had an actual chance of making a living. When I moved to New York City after college and my theater internship, only four television shows were shot there. One of them was *Sesame Street*, which introduced new human characters approximately once a decade. Meanwhile, thirty-seven television shows were filmed in Burbank. LA was where one could become a steadily working actor, and then—who knew?—maybe even a household name. After that, I could full-circle back to better stage roles in New York, because tourists who are willing to spend a hundred and sixty dollars on a Broadway ticket prefer that the show they are seeing feature familiar faces.

LA was in my future. I just needed a clearer invitation.

By my late twenties, my phone had finally rung. I'd had actual, pinch-me success as a New York theater actor, starring on Broadway as an ingenue named Sunny in *The Last Night of Ballyhoo,* a Tony Award–winning play set in the 1930s. I wore a blond wig hand-blocked to match my actual hairline that made me look like Veronica Lake. For two hundred performances I played breakup scenes at the end of Act One and happy-ending scenes at the end of Act Two, hearing audience members sniffling back their tears in the dark. My parents brought busloads of Scrantonians to see me. After a thirty-second quick change near the end of the show, I would appear at the top of a flight of stairs in a full-length blue velvet gown and long white gloves, which evoked actual gasps from the audience.

Before *Ballyhoo*'s final performance I sobbed backstage, fearing it would be the best role I would ever get to play. "You can't think that way," my costar Ilana said, and she was right, but as it turned out, so was I.

When that show ended and another leading role on Broadway was not immediately forthcoming, my agent and manager encouraged me to head to Los Angeles for the next "pilot season," which back then was an intense three-month period starting every January when all of that fall's potential TV shows would be cast. A "pilot" was a sample episode commissioned for every potential show; each network would order about twenty, film them, test them, then pick up six or so to fill in the gaps on their fall schedule.

Thousands of actors made the pilgrimage to the West Coast every year for this audition bonanza, renting studios in the famously creepy Oakwood Apartments, crisscrossing the San Fernando Valley with their headshots and their three-hundred-page bound Thomas Guide maps. The time had come for me to become one of those nomads. It was not the explicit invitation to Los Angeles I been waiting for: I had few friends there, no job, and a fiancé who would be staying back in New York City. But I had good representation, and they assured me the time was now; I had, as they explained, "some heat around me," which was not the sort of thing one could save for a later date.

I would have my first audition as soon as I landed at LAX, for the role of a ruthless television executive in a Showtime pilot. I was totally wrong for the part: the character was hard-edged and scheming and written to be in her mid-thirties, a good bit older than I was. I memorized eleven pages of dialogue on the plane and breezed into the room with zero expectations. My manager called me twenty minutes later as I was checking my mapped route to the Oakwood Apartments at a red light.

"You just got a test deal," he said.

In the movies, "screen tests" occur on an already-completed

set for the show with an actor in full hair and makeup and wardrobe. In reality, a "test" is a callback in Century City with the pilot's writer, its executive producers, and a couple of network suits all crowded into a conference room. The few actors still in the running wait in the hallway outside, pretending they can't hear one another's auditions through the paper-thin walls, pretending they aren't electrified by their proximity to monstrous possibility.

Here's what makes a test deal different from a regular callback: actors are given paperwork to sign while they wait. These contracts have been carefully vetted by their agents and lawyers and managers and business managers. The one-sidedness of these television contracts is startling: networks can terminate an actor's employment at any time and for any reason. Or for none at all. But once an actor signs her test deal, if the network chooses her—and the show makes it from pilot to series—she's pre-committed herself to that project for the next five to seven years.

The pilot I was being offered was shooting in Vancouver. There was no guarantee beyond a single episode, but if it went to series, I would be living in Vancouver for the next several years. Los Angeles was one thing—my future spouse's firm had offices there. But Vancouver was incompatible with the life I had already chosen.

I said no to the test deal.

My agents were then told that we could go right to contract; I had been their first choice.

I still said no.

This flummoxed my agents but increased my street cred as a Real New York Actor with Standards. Two weeks later I had *another* test deal, this one far too incredible to second-guess: a "series regular" role on a new sitcom, shooting in Los Angeles, working opposite a famous standup comic. This show had already passed through pilot purgatory and received a series order. If I got the part, I would be starring on prime-time television within the month.

I struggled to process how I felt about this news. I was one more audition away from my name in a show's opening credits. Which would require my living on the other side of the country from my fiancé.

My agent and manager tried to find out more about the role, since all I had to go on was the scene from my audition. The character was being added to the sitcom starting in the third episode. The show currently had only one female series regular—an Emmy winner in her mid-forties—and the word was the senior vice president of network comedy had suggested a younger female character be added for "balance." No one was suggesting the fortysomething male standup also be "balanced" with someone younger, although of course they never did. My representatives were assured the role would be significant, that whoever got the part would go toe to toe with the standup lead. I didn't feel like I was a great match for the one-sentence character description: a street-smart wisecracker who recently graduated community college. But who was I to question it? Now here I was, running my lines in the Warner Bros. reception area.

"You nervous?" a voice asked from behind me.

It was the famous comedian, the star of the show. He had wandered out of the conference room where the executives waited, probably on his way to sneak a quick smoke outside before the network tests got started.

HAPPY TO HELP

I smiled at him, trying to appear relaxed. We were alone in the waiting area; if there were other actresses testing for the role, they hadn't shown up yet. This was a very good sign.

"I guess I'm a little nervous," I admitted. I put my script on the table, realizing I'd been rolling it up in my sweaty hands. I bit down on my tongue so I wouldn't say something stupid. I wondered whether this was why the standup had come out to the waiting area—to test whether I could be cool. If I was going to match wits with him on the show each week, I couldn't seem like a fangirl. On the other hand, I shouldn't seem completely unfriendly, but I couldn't think of anything witty to say.

The standup tilted his head, squinting at me, studying me closely. This was his signature, this comedic pause of consideration. It was something I'd seen him do many times before on television: leave the other person hanging just a little longer than was comfortable. It was funny if you were watching it at home.

"Ehh, well, don't be nervous," he said finally. "And stop looking at the script. You know the lines. Just go in there."

Having said this, he walked outside to smoke.

He was right—I did know the lines. And once I knew I had the star's tacit approval, I was no longer nervous at all.

I walked into the conference room without the script and signed away the next five to seven years of my life. I got the call an hour later, standing in the parking lot of the Oakwood Apartments.

I was going to be on TV.

No Hard Feelings

A manila envelope containing the first script was hand-delivered to my doorstep that weekend. I pawed through it, looking for scenes my character was in (three) and any sense of what the show was about. The premise was that we were all social workers working for a dilapidated municipality. The standup's character was there as a condition of his sentencing for tax evasion. This made zero sense, but it would serve as a coat rack on which to hang the star's acerbic humor as he interacted with what was apparently going to be a revolving door of crazy weirdos, such as, I wish I were kidding, a homeless guy who smelled really bad.

Where did my character fit in? Her backstory remained murky; she just sort of showed up at the office in this episode and started handing out barbed insults. But my friend Jen, who'd taken college acting classes with me and had already found sitcom success in Los Angeles, told me to stop worrying about the character. This wasn't like theater. "They've hired you to play the cute one," Jen explained, a clear-enough assignment. Jen told me I needed to look camera-ready whenever I showed up on set. No sweatpants or ponytails. Hair blown out, manicure maintained.

I went to Fred Segal the next day and purchased a pink cashmere sweater for my first day on set. It had a flattering V-neck and a price tag higher than any item of clothing I'd ever owned. But since I would earn more on a single episode of this sitcom than I had after six months on Broadway, I needed to spend whatever it took to look the part.

The following Monday I drove my rental car onto the lot and was directed to a parking space with my name on it, just outside the airport-hangar-sized Stage 12. I drove past Stage 24, another block of hulking concrete, with a small *Friends* logo above its door. Jennifer Aniston was probably in there right now! She probably drove in right before I did, showing up for a new week of work just like me.

And that's when the imposter syndrome kicked in. What made me think I had a right to this job? What was I doing there?

It was a Monday, a "table read" day on multi-camera sitcoms. The script we would shoot that Friday would be read aloud by the cast for the first time, for a team of writers in one row of chairs plus the blank-faced network executives in the two behind them. I walked onto Stage 12 through a nondescript metal door. The inside was cavernous and makeshift; soundstages are usually dark and uninviting, since all the money goes into the sets rather than the workplace vibe. A few people chatted by a box of donuts on a collapsible table. They didn't look at me as I passed. Other people rushed by, busy doing jobs I didn't yet understand. There was no reception desk where I might check in. There were no signs directing me to where I belonged. I busied myself getting a cup of coffee, stirring in the powdered creamer for far longer than was necessary. Then I just stood there in my pink cashmere sweater.

"Let's get started," someone yelled out eventually. As people began to find their seats among the folding chairs, I figured out who they were based on where they were sitting. A guy in a gray hoodie turned out to be one of the executive producers. There were about eight of them, all of whom had been at my network test, although it was hard to tell which ones actually mattered; networks gave that title out like candy to agents and managers and other members of stars' entourages. But based on the seating arrangement, I could tell Guy in Hoodie was going to be one of the actual decision-makers. A woman in the power suit sat right behind him in the network row. On the table at the front, stacked with scripts, was a placard bearing my name. I sat down in front of it and waited for someone to tell me what would happen next.

A television sitcom is a weirdly siloed workplace experience. The cameramen don't hang out with wardrobe; the editors don't know the names of the makeup artists; the writers spend twelve hours a day in a tiny bungalow completely separate from the soundstage. And the actors do a lot of sitting around and waiting. It seemed like our table read went well, but as soon as it was over, people scattered in a hundred directions, leaping into action for all the work that would have to be done in the next four days. All the actors had to do was hang out and wait for the rewrites, although it was unclear to me when they'd be coming.

I knew better than to approach the star. He hadn't acknowledged me except while we were reading our scenes, and I hadn't expected more. But when lunch break was called two hours later, I saw an opening to approach the other female actor. She was the one I was really excited to be working with. She was the one I'd watched on TV for a decade. I figured I could strike up a conversation with her in the cafeteria line, hopefully join her at her table. Tell her a little about my upcoming wedding. Maybe I'd even invite her. After all, we'd be working together every day.

"Hey. Hi. I'm just wondering, where do we all go for lunch?" I asked her.

"You know, we all mostly do our own thing," she said. Then she went into her dressing room and closed the door.

HAPPY TO HELP

In film and television production, actors are more commonly referred to as "the *talent*," the emphasis on the word possessing major eye-roll energy. Even famous actors fail to receive the same breathless level of interest on set as they do everywhere else. If the lead actor is someone who was famous before their current show—or if the show they're on has already run for several seasons—the lead is also a producer, off making decisions whenever they're not camera-blocking a scene. But the rest of the actors, even the household names, just show up to do their jobs. Know your lines. Don't talk when the director is talking. Hit your mark—your taped X on the floor—so your shot won't be out of focus.

Most important: don't be the reason everyone has to do it all again.

I felt like I was sufficiently checking all those boxes, but it was hard to tell. The star of the show still hadn't spoken to me since the day of my test, except in character and during a scene. During our frequent downtime he liked to hang around behind the cameras with the director of most of the episodes, who usually had an unlit cigar in his mouth. The raucousness of their laughter did not seem to indicate conversations in which outsiders, particularly female ones, would be warmly welcomed. I started to see why the other female actor spent so much time in her dressing room.

Wednesday afternoons were network run-throughs, when we'd stumble through a staged version of a script that had been almost completely rewritten since Monday's table read. The writers, producers, and network suits moved as a pack from set to set, fake-laughing where it was hoped the studio audience would, circling those spots in the script to make sure there were at least two laughs per page. They'd confer afterward while the actors stood around. Then Guy in Hoodie would give notes and corrections before we all were sent home.

When I didn't receive any notes the first week, I was thrilled. No notes! I was doing a great job! When it happened a couple of weeks in a row, I began to question it. To myself, that is. Not getting feedback could mean that I was doing exactly what the executive producers wanted. That there was nothing I had to fix. On the other hand, it was hard to read being ignored on set as entirely positive.

It was another executive producer who finally pulled me aside halfway through my fourth week on set: Cynthia, the most senior female working on Stage 12, clear second-in-command to Guy in Hoodie. If he wanted something to happen, it was up to Cynthia to make sure it did.

She gestured for me to join her behind one of the sets. I'd never had a one-on-one conversation with her and was delighted to finally be receiving her attention. On this male-dominated set, it might be Cynthia with whom I could finally connect.

"So. That accent you're doing," she said. In my audition I had made a vague gesture toward a tough-girl accent, like Jo from *The Facts of Life*. Since they had cast me, I figured I was supposed to keep it up, and had done so for the first three episodes. "We're going to drop it."

"Oh! Okay, sure!" I said, all reasonable flexibility, a team player. "How are we planning to explain the change?" This was network television, after all; continuity would obviously be required. I imagined a *My Fair Lady* B-plot with tons of scenes for my character, rife with comic possibility.

HAPPY TO HELP

Cynthia stared at me. "You're . . . just not going to do it anymore," she said with a shrug, before walking away to talk to someone far more interesting.

⌒

As the weeks went by, my role got smaller and smaller. By my fifth episode, my contribution was to answer the phone, say "Hello? Yeah, he's right here," hand it to the standup, then stand there while he and another actor exchanged quips about my character's probable past in the porn industry.

I reminded myself how many actresses would kill to be in my place. I was still receiving billing in the opening credits. Still making more in a week than I had in a year as a personal assistant. Our ratings were good, and word was the show was getting picked up for another season. I would have the whole summer off to get married. Jennifer Aniston was still two soundstages over.

But something wasn't working. I had to figure out what it was and turn things around, because I couldn't quit. My contract didn't allow it. And I didn't want to spend the next five years this way. I had to convince at least some of the people in charge—the star, the executive producers, the network suits—that I deserved more attention.

I started going to extra lunchtime spinning classes on the lot, sweating next to Brooke Shields, then carefully redoing my makeup in my dressing room. I hung out on set during breaks instead of hiding in my dressing room, talking to whomever might make eye contact. I began lurking around the edges of "video village" when we shot before live audiences, eavesdropping on the decision-makers in their directors' chairs as they squinted at the playback on the monitors.

But no one was saying anything bad about me. No one was saying anything about me at all.

Halfway through the week we shot my sixth episode, the wardrobe department asked me if I wouldn't mind sticking around after our network run-through. "We have some new looks for your character," the costume designer said. "Cynthia wants to take a look."

This had to be a good sign. I'd never seen Cynthia in makeup or wardrobe once. If she was turning her attention toward the way my character looked, that had to mean my future on the show held promise. Maybe I had finally proven myself worthy of consideration.

I reported to wardrobe after rehearsal to find a large rack of outfits pulled for me to try on, a far larger range than usual. Everything was fresh from Nordstrom, tags still attached.

Cynthia pulled up a folding chair next to the rack.

"Oh, okay, Cynthia, you want to sit there?" the costume designer said, obviously rearranging how this would go on the fly. This wasn't a usual visit. "That's totally fine. In that case, Amy, why don't you change in my office?"

"No, that's okay," Cynthia said. "She can change right here."

The costume designer and I both froze. Were we supposed to be okay with the producer watching me change? If Cynthia were a guy, it would clearly be creepy. She wasn't a man, so . . . maybe it was just a little weird? But Cynthia was also one of my bosses, so I changed right there.

I had not foreseen the requirements of the "cute one" extending to my lingerie. I hunched over as I stripped down, hoping I was obscuring Cynthia's view of my frumpy Wacoal minimizer bra, my stretched-out underpants.

Cynthia tilted her head at each new outfit I tried on, her lack of enthusiasm evident, although she did not say what it was that was disappointing her. The flop-sweating costume designer handed me hangers faster and faster, forcing me to give up all pretense of modesty in order to change quicker, until finally I found myself standing before the executive producer half-naked, in my grandma bra and sensible underwear, while the costume designer futzed with a zipper.

Cynthia looked my body up and down, her eyes pausing on my lower half. On my exposed thighs, which had always been, ever since my days of reading *Young Miss*, just a little bigger than I'd liked. Thighs that had resisted my repeated attempts at spot-reducing. Thighs that, when seen this close up, were definitely not Hollywood-ready.

"How—*old* are you?" Cynthia asked, staring at my bare legs with evident repulsion.

With a sudden, hot shame I understood what the problem had been all along, and why she'd wanted to be in the room while I changed: a suspicion that, underneath all the hair and makeup and wardrobe, I was insufficiently attractive. Cynthia had been dispatched to do a little strategic observation. And here my thighs were, giving up the game.

"I'm twenty-eight," I said, suddenly finding it hard to make any sound at all. This was a lie: I was twenty-nine. In my panic I desperately lied about my age, but by only a year, hoping if I could convince Cynthia I was three percent less old, I'd be three percent less All Wrong. How old had they all thought I was? I was pretty sure my employer wasn't legally allowed to ask me my age—let alone see me in my underwear—but I had been stunned into nearly complete candor by Cynthia's disgust.

I'd been caught being almost thirty. It felt close to unforgivable.

I relived this exchange in my head all weekend long at the Oakwood Apartments. My tiny studio had a Murphy bed that took up most of the room at night but folded up into a wall during the day. That wall's surface was fully mirrored, presumably to make the apartment seem larger and brighter and less lonely. When the bed was up, I couldn't be anywhere in my apartment without seeing my reflection. I bought wrapping paper and tape at the grocery store, enough for me to cover the entire wall.

We shot the last episode of the season two weeks later. Guy in Hoodie came up to me at the wrap party as I stood to one side playing with a frilled toothpick.

"So, what are your plans this summer?" he asked.

"I'm getting married," I said.

"Wow! Are you?" he said. (I had definitely mentioned this previously.)

"Uh, yes. Next month. What are you doing this summer?"

"Getting out of here. Going on a four-week cruise. Can't wait," he said. "But, hey, you know, about your wedding? Let me give you a little bit of advice I wish someone had told me when I first got married: it doesn't have to be forever."

I started to laugh, thinking that was my job, like it was one of our run-throughs and someone standing nearby would circle it in the script. *Laugh track goes here.* But by the way he then clapped my back in friendly farewell, I realized he meant it.

People get fired all the time in Hollywood. They never call it that, of course. When your manager calls to break the news, they give the same feedback as when you weren't wanted in the first place: the people who hired you are going in another direction.

An actor under contract is not allowed to declare she's leaving, but those in charge can decide hiring her was a mistake and then drop her without ever having to explain why.

The producers had prearranged a time to call my manager's office. I sat there in the office, waiting for the phone to ring, so Guy in Hoodie could tell me this news personally. I was told this was very nice of him, since he had had to arrange a ship-to-shore phone call from his cruise to do so. Maybe it was. I was getting more attention from him now than I had while I was working on his show.

"I just wanted to thank you so much for your lovely work," he said on the call, "and to let you know that we're going in another direction."

"Yes, I had heard that," I said.

"It's always a tough thing."

"It's okay," I said. Now I wouldn't have to spend the next several years wondering if I was doing a good job. Now I could get married and not have to leave a month later. It was as okay as losing a major television role could be. I mostly just wanted to get off the phone. "Well. Thank you for calling."

"Hold on, there's a little bit more," he said. "And I wanted you to hear it from me."

There had been a different actress originally cast in the pilot. Because she was unavailable when the show got picked up, they had created my character and hired me. Now that other show had been canceled, meaning they'd be able to recast that original actress in this sitcom after all. She'd be replacing me as the cute one, playing the same character as she had in the pilot: a sarcastic hooker with a heart of gold.

That actress was nineteen.

Three years later, after I moved back to New York City for good, I got a call from an old friend. He'd been my writing partner for a romantic comedy that almost sold and earned us a meeting with a literary agent, who said if we really wanted to work in the business, we needed to move to LA. "Los Angeles is where things happen," the agent said.

Maybe it was, but not for me, not anymore. I was pregnant with my first child by then. My former writing partner, free of such encumbrances, had moved to Los Angeles without me. The day he called, he had a question. "I'm reading this book that goes behind the scenes on TV shows," he said. "And I'm not sure, but . . . I think you might be in it?"

It turned out a journalist had been embedded with my sitcom while I was on it, though I couldn't recall ever having seen such a person on set. He had then written a book called *The Showrunners*, which chronicled the ups and downs of several new sitcoms that season. (The title was a Hollywood-insider nickname for the executive producers who actually run the shows.)

The Showrunners explained what had happened in my sitcom's writer's room—the bungalow actors were not allowed to enter—when the idea for my character had first been introduced:

> *Talk turns to a pressing matter—the addition of a currently unnamed and unformed younger female character suggested by the network. Everyone in the room has taken to referring to this mystery woman as "Trixie La Boom Boom." Is breathing life into Trixie something the writers want to do, or something they have to do?*
> "We have to," said the star.
> "*We* want *to have to*," said the showrunner.

I was horrified: *Trixie La Boom Boom?* Me? I had taken Intro to Women's Studies! Despite all my high-minded notions of how my acting career would play out, I had accepted a role as a tits-and-ass caricature. Had the character description said what they were really looking for I would never have agreed to the audition, let alone the role.

Worse still, everyone on set but me had known the truth about Trixie, and no wonder everyone had hated her: the writers who had no intention of writing material for her, the other female actor insulted by her existence, the female wardrobe designer who was pulling her hair out, the female executive producer who had to do reconnaissance work to figure out whether I was hot enough.

My presence on set had been a reminder—to everyone but me—that their show had been deemed unworthy without the addition of a jailbait sex kitten. And then I wasn't even very good at it. If my assignment was to become Trixie La Boom Boom, I had been horribly miscast. I was young and pretty and thin, if not Hollywood skinny, but I wasn't *that*. It was like hiring Kidz Bop for a bachelor party.

I had spent months trying to understand what I was doing wrong so that I could fix it. It was far longer before I would accept that I never could have, not even if I went the extra mile, not even if I kept running forever.

If I had learned that truth sooner, would that have changed anything? It might have been worse. I would have still had to show up for work every day, far unhappier, under a contract that did not allow me to quit. Though I can't imagine anyone would have stopped me if I'd tried.

Being Trixie La Boom Boom had never been a life goal of mine. Learning that I'd been fired for *not* being her actually brought me a sense of peace. There was nothing I could have done differently except to have said no in the first place, to an offer that at the time seemed far too good to refuse.

I never watched the sitcom after that, although it would run for two more seasons with its replacement Trixie. *Maxim* magazine said she had "knockout knockers." I honestly wished her well. And I would remain grateful for my first television show, which taught me well how Hollywood worked, and, as it turned out, without significant damage to my own prospects: I would be cast on another sitcom within a couple of months. If Hollywood loves chewing actors up, if it enforces outrageous sexism and ageism, it also has the shortest of memories. This was why my tough-cookie character could disappear from the show that was supposed to be my introduction to Hollywood without anyone besides me really caring or asking why.

It might also be why the book that memorialized that strange time in my life got the Trixie La Boom Boom details correct, but also got my last name wrong.

Look on the Bright Side

When people describe their younger years, they often begin with the blanket disclaimer that their mother was a saint, and everyone listening understands what is meant. When someone says, "My mother was a saint!" they are implying that their own past behavior, and that of their siblings—and perhaps even their other parent's as well—gave their mother many sleepless nights, but that she withstood it all with the tolerance of someone just a little too good to be a regular human like the rest of us.

Whether the storyteller's history included coming home past curfew singing power ballads, or repeated calls from the principal's office—or both—their maternal figure is understood to have absorbed all unpleasantness without complaint, utilizing great reserves of long-sufferance. "My mother was a *saint*," some erstwhile rascal will say, chuckling and shaking his head in rueful acknowledgment of the *tsuris* he put his mother through. And then everyone else will laugh: Ho ho, don't they know it! They could tell a few stories of their own—they put their mothers through the wringer too!

One does not have to be religious or a former hoodlum to call their mother a saint. I've certainly called my own mother one.

But what you'll never hear—or at least I never have—is someone making the same sort of observation about a male parent. Forbearance during trials of patience is not a traditional part of a father's job description.

Sometimes what we torment our mothers with is less dramatic troublemaking than everyday psychological baggage. "Our teenagers lighten their loads by passing their problems to us," psychologist Lisa Damour explains, calling what teens tend to hand parents their "emotional trash." Studies have shown that mothers are the preferred garbage receptacle. Adolescents of all genders have been shown to be more likely to direct verbal abuse at their mothers than at their fathers, romantic interests, or friends. That might be because most of us believe female parents to be more capable of the self-restraint required in response. One of my own teenagers enjoys ending our own discussions about exactly what they plan to do all summer by shouting, "Mom, why do you always *ruin everything*?" before going off to have a pleasant-enough afternoon looking at their phone. Having discharged this negative emotion onto me, my child feels great; once emotional trash is handed over, it's generally forgotten. At least by the adolescent.

But I used to give as good as I now get. I remember sitting on the piano bench in the dining room of my childhood home and telling my mother she was the actual, literal Wicked Witch of the West for making me practice, thereby gaining the emotional buoyancy to play "Joy to the World" *allegro maestoso* immediately afterward. Bright and cheerful. Christmas was on its way—who among us wasn't merry? I certainly was, letting nothing me dismay, having handed that grouchy unpleasantness over for my mother to deal with. She really was a saint.

Look on the Bright Side

It's amazing, really, how mothers have the strength to hold all the nonsense we hand them, whether it's flirtations with juvenile delinquency or devastation after a messy breakup. Mothers never externalize messy emotions like that themselves, at least not if they're good at their jobs. While taking on the sorrowful burdens of others, it is additionally crucial that a mother never show just how hard that work can be.

That work, by the way, is something a mother will be doing most of the time, due to another truth universally acknowledged: a mother is never allowed to be happy when one of her children is not.

My husband and I recently ran into an old friend, a father of three who seemed diminished and sad. When we asked him how he was doing, he told us very little about himself and a great deal about his middle child's struggles. "Well, you know what they say," he concluded. "You're only as happy as your unhappiest child."

"God, that's true," my husband said, and remarked to me on the drive home how his old friend's statement had really stuck with him. What a good point it was.

I couldn't believe my husband hadn't heard that hundreds of times before. For me, that saying had been fully integrated—part adage, part assignment.

Five years earlier I had been diverted away from my daughter's hospital bed by the pediatric chief resident, who took me for an out-of-earshot stroll to explain that my daughter was going to be discharged despite her unabated and excruciating pain. Over the course of a month, what had started as a barely twisted left ankle had become a leg on which my ten-year-old could put no weight. By the time I got her to the orthopedist a few days after the injury, it had become a boot of pain, purple and cold, overtaking my daughter's leg from her toes to her knee, even though the X-rays showed no visible damage.

That orthopedist had also taken me out in the hallway. "I don't want to alarm you," she said, which of course is always perfectly alarming, "but there's this thing. It's really rare. And if that's what this is, I won't be able to help her."

It was, and she couldn't. As this orthopedist suspected, my daughter's actual affliction—complex regional pain syndrome (CRPS)—was originating in her nervous system rather than in her ankle. The bones and tendons were sound, but my daughter's brain was stuck sending five-alarm pain signals. It was as if the sudden, sharp pain you get from pinching a finger in a door hinge—there to make you pay immediate attention but then quickly subside—instead got slowly, increasingly worse.

On the McGill Pain Index, used to rate patient pain, CRPS ranks at the very top—more than kidney stones, more than unmedicated childbirth, more than amputation. My daughter's leg had become so agonizing that sitting on the edge of her hospital bed caused her to cry out. Her whole body would shake with anticipatory fear when it was time to help her to the bathroom. After two days, all the medications the hospital deemed safe enough for a fourth-grader hadn't helped at all. She was gray and weak, and I was bursting into tears anytime someone with a clipboard entered her room.

"Let's take a walk, Mom," the chief resident said.

I bristled. *Mom.* How patronizing. Couldn't he just have used my name? Or simply asked me what my name *was*, since he'd obviously never bothered to learn it in the first place?

There was a room down the hall with a hand-lettered sign on the door designating it for "Child Life." Neither child-occupied nor lively, it was the perfect place for a conversation guaranteed to remain private. The resident invited me to sit on a tiny chair next to a bin of broken crayons and a play kitchen without accessories. He waited for me to take several deep breaths.

"I know this is hard to accept, but we've done everything we can," he finally explained. "Your daughter's recovery will be a long process, and you're the one who's going to make it happen."

"You can't just *send her home* like this," I said, weeping freely into my sweatshirt. "I have no idea how to help her! She can't even *walk*."

"The only way she will walk is if you make her do it. Even if she's in incredible pain. If this is ever going to get better, it's going to be up to you, Mom."

There it was again. *Mom.* Perhaps he intended it as an honorific. An acknowledgment of a title that, just like his own, I had earned after years of hard work. A title that signified that it was indeed up to me. I would have to help my daughter heal without possessing either road map or confidence that I could do so. And, just as a stakes-raiser for this Ultimate Mom Gladiator Challenge, I could never let my child see how worried I was.

~

Natalia Imperatori-Lee has written about the emotional labor of mothers in Latin American cultures, and how they perform mourning rituals in the name of their families succeeding. These women offer daily works of worry as sacrifice, in order that their loved ones might suffer less. These devotions are usually home-based and Catholic in nature: rosaries, black mantillas, and particular devotion to the Virgin Mary, Our Lady of Sorrows, venerated above all others for her example of patient grief. What woman could be more lovely?

I haven't owned a rosary since my First Communion, but when I heard about these "mourning rituals" I recognized my own, in both the "sad" and "early in the day" senses of the word. When I get up before my family to box-breathe, suffer through pigeon pose, or even do an "XOXO Cody" ride on the Peloton, I am performing my own home-based devotions. I might categorize all these things as self-care, as small indulgences of me-time. But if you asked me why I did them, I would explain it was so I could show up as the best parent and partner I could be. That I really did all these things for the people I love.

My husband would probably not say he golfs so he can be a better parent and partner, to become a more enlightened version of the person he needs to be. I think he'd say he golfs because he enjoys it. If more patience and peacefulness come along with it, that's certainly welcome, but it's not what motivates him to play. When I lay out my yoga mat, light a candle, set an intention, there is part of me that hopes the feelings I release might allow the ones I love to float more peacefully above their own burdens. There's a part of me that believes my work of worry can set them free.

If I've gotten pretty woo-woo since my parochial school upbringing, I've come by it honestly. Once I finally got my daughter into the recommended pediatric pain clinic, they in turn

Look on the Bright Side

referred her to a holistic health care provider, who then proposed a neuromuscular reeducation specialist, who then suggested energy work. These suggestions were always offered hesitantly, as if I were going to say no, as if I wouldn't have signed my daughter up for a sound-bathing oxygen chamber in a minute if someone said it might work.

I took my daughter to acupuncture and craniosacral therapy, introduced her to meditation and Jin Shin Jyutsu. I learned self-healing strategies alongside her as a means to encourage her, wrapping the palm of my hand around the thumb of the other to harmonize my energy functions. Together we would breathe in for four, out for six. I kept these things up long after my daughter discarded them as not working well enough. They worked for me.

It was only much later that I wondered why that chief resident didn't ask my husband to join us in the Child Life room that day. Why only one parent had been summoned and then assigned what felt impossible: making a sick child well when an entire hospital could not.

Maybe the doctor thought someone should stay with my daughter. Maybe he quickly decided that my husband was the better person for that job, since he wasn't ugly-crying in front of her like I was. And maybe the doctor assumed that, as the mother, I would be taking on this work of worry, and I would be doing so alone.

I certainly assumed the same. I never thought to ask if we might pause that conversation to have my husband join us, if only to hold my hand. I never considered whether my spouse might stay overnight with our son for his sleep study, or talk to his doctors about trying another medication. I accepted this work as mine and only mine, and then bristled whenever my husband would say, about any of our children's struggles, that he was going to take it one day at a time. That he was choosing to feel confident everything would work out okay. *I'm the reason you get to think that!* I wanted to shout. *You get to be optimistic because I'm holding all the hard stuff.*

But I also never came out and asked if those emotional and practical burdens might be shared. Getting my children better—and holding all the fear that it might not work—was my job. The greater my children's burdens, the more crucial my work of worry was. The greater my emotional burdens, the better a mother I would be.

Or so I thought.

I didn't possess the beautiful, sad acceptance of the *Pietà*. I wasn't always a perfect Giving Tree. When it would all get to be too much—when my work of worry boiled over into irritability or anger—my family would be baffled by whatever escaped my personal volcano. It hadn't been apparent I was struggling. I hadn't asked for support. They weren't even sure what I was so upset about, since I was usually pretty good at keeping the pattern of their daily lives smooth and undisturbed.

It's when those of us who do the work of worry are most exhausted and despondent, when we finally ask for help, that we will be told that we could instead just stop worrying and choose to believe that everything will work out fine.

And maybe it will. If the work of worry shouldn't be undertaken by women alone, does that mean those around us have to do more of it? Or does it mean that work doesn't need to be done by anyone at all?

Sometimes worry is like gripping the armrest on a turbulent

plane, willing it to remain in the air. Rationally, we understand that our flight path will be equally unaltered by passenger 8A's panic, passenger 8B's prayers to St. Joseph of Cupertino, patron saint of air travelers, and passenger 8C's decision that the pilots probably know what they're doing so he'll just keep watching *Yellowstone*.

But some of us are going to pray anyhow. Some of us are going to grip the armrests.

And some of us are the pilots flying through the thunderstorms.

There's a big difference between habitual middle-of-the-night ruminations about all the bad things that might happen to the ones we love and the night when the phone actually rings. At those times, those of us who do the work of worry are not lesser or weaker for doing it. But we are also not less worthy whenever we are able to worry less.

The pain specialists prescribed a gradual but forced return to normalcy for my daughter. In order to reset the overdrive in which her central nervous system was stuck, she would have to do—a little bit at a time—what her brain was telling her was impossible. After a week's concentrated effort, she could withstand my dragging a single Post-it note back and forth across her lower leg. Once that amount of contact was possible, her next challenge was to sit with both feet flat on the floor. After a few more weeks, she was using crutches. Then a walker, then a cane. The pain would never have left if she lay there waiting for it to go. She had to fully experience each painful moment of using her leg in order to show her brain that it was safe to do so.

HAPPY TO HELP

It was just the same for me: I had to force myself to find small moments, then larger ones, where I could exist without the worry. First I had to forgive myself for crying at the sound of the kids running and shouting on the playground out our apartment window when my own child was in too much pain to go outside. Then I had to forgive myself for going out into that same sunshine without her, for taking a walk with a friend. For having moments, and then entire afternoons, when I managed to forget.

If part of me believed my work of worrying could relieve my children's suffering, another part of me feared that anything I did to ease my own burdens might make them suffer more. But as I looked back, no matter which child was taking their turn as my unhappiest, they did not suffer less when I worried about them more. I would never find freedom from worry if I waited for the worry to disappear.

I was not only as worthy as my unhappiest child.

—⁓—

"It is an act of immense generosity to be the architect of everyone else's well-being," Deborah Levy has written. "This task is still mostly perceived as women's work." By women as well: we've internalized messages that self-sacrifice equals care, that suffering equals love, that we can keep bad things from happening to those we love by worrying that they will. We accept these burdens readily. We're made for this work. It's not like anyone else wants to become the keeper of what's hard. So who's supposed to hold this stuff? *No one?*

Perhaps.

Prayer might change outcomes. I'd like to think it does. But it's hard to argue the same about worry. We can't protect those we love through uncertain times with the power of our minds. But it's pretty hard to accompany them through those times of uncertainty without our minds coming along.

I had to call two dozen physical therapists before I found someone who knew how to work with complex regional pain syndrome. I carried my daughter into Saul's office from the taxi on my back for her first appointment. Saul was always in a good mood, upbeat and encouraging, cheering my daughter on every time she made the smallest progress, pretending not to notice when I would leave the room wiping my eyes. Seeing Saul treat her so confidently allowed me to hope all would be well.

Four months later, she walked across the room without her cane.

Saul called me a month or so after her last appointment to follow up. "You wouldn't believe it," I said. "She's walking to school. She might start taking ballet again! Saul, you told me to keep the faith, and you were right."

"Well, I can tell you this now," Saul said. "Before she first came in, since I'd never worked on a case like this before, I called around to get some advice. One guy told me it would take her a year and a half to walk again. The other guy told me to run the other way, because it would probably never happen at all."

I never knew Saul had less than complete confidence that she was on the right path. That lack of knowledge gave me such hope. In the same way, my hiding the depths of my worry from my child had to have helped her become well again sooner.

When we have to do the work of worry, hiding it might be a necessary part of the job.

But am I supposed to hide my work of worry from everyone? Am I always to walk through difficult times acting like what I'm carrying isn't heavy? I can't accept that a mother's true path to a deserving life is always to worry more and show it less. But sometimes I'm not sure what to do instead.

Back when my daughter's pain was basically all I thought about, I threw her walker into the back of our car and drove her to Boston for a parent-child weekend intensive for kids with chronic pain. A teenager who had "graduated" from the same program spoke to us, describing her own recovery from gastrointestinal pain so severe it had required a feeding tube to life as a typical high school senior. She and her mother were there to tell us that such a successful outcome, with continued physiological and psychological support, could someday be possible for all our children, no matter how far away it felt at the time.

I recently asked my daughter if she'd like to go back and offer that same graduate speech, paying it forward to the next group of suffering children and their suffering parents.

"I guess we could go," she answered. Then she said, "I feel like I don't remember that time all that well. I mean, it's been almost five years. That was a long time ago."

My child doesn't really remember the extent of her suffering. I will never really forget.

Years from now, will my daughter smile at the memory of me carrying her into Saul's office and say, "Let me tell you, my mother was a saint"? I guess I hope she won't. I hope my daughter will remember all of me, not just my forced cheeriness and swallowed frustration, but also my morning stupor before I had my coffee, the incessant and irritating habit I had of talking in our dog's imaginary voice, my irrational impatience whenever we had to wait in line.

I hope I will have modeled for my children the holiness of all our everyday actions: when we worry but also when we laugh; when we pray, and when we sleep soundly through the night.

It's Never Too Late

A friend of mine recently mentioned her waning energy levels on Facebook, with the wry and obligatory aside that her increasing fatigue was no doubt due to her advancing age. In the comments, a mutual acquaintance told my friend to follow a certain influencer on Instagram. "She just so *gets* women our age," this person raved, and although I'd never heard of this influencer, because I love taking the advice of strangers on the internet, I clicked right over to Instagram and hit "follow" so that I, too, could live a more energetic life.

Twenty-four hours later, that same influencer had appeared in my feed a dozen times, utilizing exuberant short videos and snazzy infographics to inform me that I was pooping incorrectly. According to this influencer, a woman my age was supposed to be moving her bowels not just daily, but *two to three times* daily, and anyone who wasn't was doing it wrong.

Let's just say I was getting that assignment very, very wrong.

Let's just say you presume I'm what some might call retentive, and I'll presume that wasn't already obvious to you.

There was so much else I'd been neglecting to consider. This influencer cheerily prescribed a complete "life reset" for her several hundred thousand perimenopausal followers. Since what came out was obviously affected by what was going in, a woman my age also needed to track her protein, eating at least 120 grams per day from a proper variety of sources. I had no idea how much protein I ate in a day, but a quick perusal of the hyperlinked supporting materials indicated that after counting the protein in what I was currently eating—a protein bar—I would only have to find another 108 grams by nightfall.

After spending an entire day distracted by internet searches on how to source regular deliveries of organic bone broth, I unfollowed this influencer, immediately feeling that boost of energy I had been seeking in the first place. It wasn't that I doubted that her advice might work; her vibrancy and dewiness fairly leaped out from my phone screen. It was that I sensed my following her instructions would lead less to a younger me with greater energy levels and more to a lot of time feeling bad about myself because I wasn't pooping enough.

If there's one thing I thought getting older would grant me, it was increasing acceptance of my increasing limitations. When I was a kid and we'd go to the town pool, I was always fascinated by the ladies who gathered to chat in the shallow end. I knew to keep my distance; these ladies did not appreciate their beauty shop wash-and-sets being splashed. They did not, it seemed, want to swim at all. But these women spent entire afternoons in the water, laughing and talking, blocking the steps like the whole pool was theirs. I wondered what was so funny. I figured they were laughing because they had outlived the concerns of regular grown-ups. They could stop worrying about looking old, because they did, which meant these women were free to start living their best lives.

I thought I'd naturally feel that same middle-aged freedom once I got there. But these days, whenever I come across a photo of one of my female ancestors squinting unsmilingly in her back yard, I do the math, then gasp. "Great-Great-Great-Nana is only four years older than me in this picture!" I tell my children, sure they will share my shock that this scowling, aproned nonna could have anything at all in common with their vital and hip mother.

My children are never quite as surprised as I'd like them to be.

Now that I've reached Lady at the Town Pool age, what I'd always presumed would be an unavoidable and therefore easy assignment—giving my older self the gift of acceptance—has shifted. In a world where everything can be hacked and tracked, we are invited to give constant focus to upgrading and enhancing even the most ordinary parts of our daily lives. To lean in to longevity. And that assignment doesn't just apply to women.

My husband has recently taken up rucking. When he announced this was happening, I assumed a mountain and some sort of ice axe would be involved. Turns out rucking is actually just plain old walking, while wearing a specialized backpack weighted down with metal plates. Rucking was originally developed by the military to prepare soldiers for the times they might have to carry everything they own on their backs for long distances. While my husband passed the upper age limit for a Navy Seal a couple of decades ago, he now enjoys rucking around our neighborhood with at least thirty additional pounds strapped to his back, I suppose so that if things should change and he is suddenly summoned to the western Pacific, he'll be prepared. He doesn't tell me his motivations, and I for sure don't ask. My husband and I have a tacit agreement: he may "ruck" while we walk the dog, but I will neither acknowledge he is wearing a forty-pound metal plate (with ergonomic lumbar support) as we do so, nor listen to why the neuroscientist he follows on Spotify thinks I should be doing it too. I don't *want* to hear about the cool new way a few intense dudes have discovered to make even walking extreme and unpleasant. Besides, I've already spent months of my life with about forty extra pounds on me—three times, as a matter of fact, and mostly out in front, which offered far less in the way of that lumbar support.

My spouse swears by rucking's benefits though. He knows it's working because he monitors his recovery rate. And his respiratory rate. And his REM sleep. And there must be something to it all, because my husband is more visibly fit today than he was when I met him almost thirty years ago. But it's not vanity that is driving his focus on these markers of his health, although his BMI is enviable. My spouse is motivated by the fit and mobile eighty-year-old he is aiming to be. Each time he lifts something even moderately heavy, or stretches his Achilles while we wait for the elevator, he reminds me that he's thinking about the quality of life he wants to have thirty years from now, the grandchildren he wants to be able to keep up with.

To me that's a long game, but I'd be lying if I said I never listened. And my husband isn't the only one talking about it. The culture of optimization offers opportunities for continual self-tinkering, making endless excellent tiny choices to make our bodies stronger, or at least delay their getting weaker. In return we get the most precious gift of all—more time on Earth—but only by fixing everything we're currently doing wrong.

Because we're doing it *all* wrong. We're brushing our hair

wrong: if we're not using a boar-bristled brush and starting from the bottom, we may be causing scalp damage. We're drinking our coffee wrong: if we're not waiting ninety minutes after waking to drink it, we may be disrupting our natural cortisol patterns. We're sleeping wrong, unless our resting heart rate exhibits, when graphed, the proper hammock pattern. We're *breathing* wrong. Were we out of our minds, thinking we could just breathe without even thinking about it?

These days my social media feeds and Substack subscriptions offer daily admonishments about how someone my age really needs to kick it all into a higher gear, because I really don't have a moment to lose. Not when I'm losing muscle mass right now, when my brain is shrinking *right now*. Not when there are projects of self-betterment I could be undertaking instead of reading the newsletter listing them all.

And the more unpleasant the life hack is, the more virtuous and essential its wellness-enhancing claims are. An ice bath sounds horrific, but how else am I going to form the correct kind of fat, which, as I have just learned, is brown and not white? How else am I going to shock my mordant metabolism back into twentysomething condition if not by actively shivering that lymph right out of my system?

I want to laugh at all of this. I want all of this to be a waste of time. But my friend Lauren, a year or so older than I am, just completed her first triathlon and has signed up to do another one. I am consistently presented with evidence suggesting it is not too late at all. That growing old does not need to mean I stop caring.

And so sometimes I do buy in. I try the one piece of athletic equipment that will completely transform my workout, the one ingredient that will supercharge my smoothies. I used to make fun of my husband for letting his perception of a good night's sleep be ruined by what his Whoop told him. Now the first thing I check in the morning is my Fitbit, so I can find out whether my sleep was Good or just Fair. With an average score of 79.3, my Fitbit is giving me the worst grades I've ever gotten, in a marking period that will last the rest of my life—unless I stop checking, thereby renouncing any hope of a healthier me.

Fitness and longevity don't have finish lines. The eternal hard work is the point, although at least all decision-making can be handed over to the algorithm. This is why full-time lifehackers like Bryan Johnson (364K followers on Instagram) always eat dinner alone: when you're spending two million dollars a year to disrupt your own aging process, you are obligated to eat your last meal of the day at eleven a.m. "Who'd want to date me?" Johnson jokes, but the joylessness of his daily oblations seems to be the thing he's most proud of.

Still, the influencers who undertake these ceaseless and extremely expensive labors of youthification don't exactly look younger. They look more preserved, like frogs floating in formaldehyde. Longevity aficionados usually look like you have no idea how old they are, and maybe that is the point. Meredith Jones calls this new ideal "stretched middle age," and says those who seek it live on a hamster wheel chasing "constant projects of self-betterment." Even those of us who dismiss it all as far too much work still have to do the small but perpetual work of resisting it. If I read a headline telling me there's one thing I need to do right now to retain muscle, but then choose *not* to count my macros, it is with a tiny ping of awareness that that too is a choice, one meaning I may indeed die a bit sooner. Or at least be infinitesimally less healthy. If I do attempt these eternal projects of self-betterment, any moment not spent counting my macros will feel like cheating, and I'll still be exhausted—by the daily small failures of my body continuing to grow older anyhow, the odometer stubbornly refusing to stop its roll.

You might indeed be able to slow the visible markers of the aging process, but you can't slow down time. Anyone old enough to feel old will swear that time feels like it starts to move faster. It may be true: philosopher Paul Janet suggested that the subjective rate of time passing increases in proportion to the age of the person making the assessment. That would explain why a five-year-old perceives a year as a very long time; it represents twenty percent of the life she has lived so far. For a fifty-year-old, that same year equals two percent of the road behind. It's log time. The longer we live, the faster it goes, as our lives hurtle toward a finish line we will reach no matter how many antioxidants we take.

That is why, despite my type-A-ing just about every other part of my life, I am trying not to lean in to longevity. I don't want to close my fitness rings in order to feel like a good person. I don't want to improve my metabolic age. I don't want to know what my metabolic age *is*. I want some things about myself to be truly fine just as they already are. If neuroinflammation leads to more rapid brain aging, so does obsessing about neuroinflammation. So does living another year.

In my head, of course, I am someone much younger. Looking out through my own eyes, I experience the world as the same me I have always been, forgetting just how much time has passed. I can remember learning how to water-ski like it was yesterday, and have to do actual math to realize that day was almost forty years ago. While I waited, shivering, on the dock of a lake in the Poconos, I was instructed that when my turn came I should lock my arms straight, keep my ski tips up, and let the boat pull me. That was all there was to it. But like most novices, as soon as I was pulled out of the water I attempted to help myself stay up, bending my elbows and pulling the tow rope closer to me. The boat driver decelerated as soon as I made this rookie mistake, meaning the faceplant I took was at least more embarrassing than painful.

I was given another chance. This time I chose to accept what I was being told: all I had to do was be pulled through the water. All I had to do was nothing.

After a few moments moving over the water, I realized I was doing it.

After a few more moments, it was even almost enjoyable: moving faster and faster, leaning back, looking up at the sky.

Cherish Every Moment

On a late winter Manhattan evening a few years ago, my husband and I squeezed into an auditorium with a few hundred fellow parents of high school juniors. Awaiting us on each seat were red binders with a cover cartoon image of Calvin and Hobbes, the irrepressible youngster and his real-life tiger companion. It was a cultural reference pegged more closely to my own adolescence than to my child's, although that might have been the intention.

In the cartoon, Calvin and Hobbes were pictured hurtling joyfully downhill in a red toy wagon, doing the sort of manifestly unsafe thing kids get to do only when not under adult supervision. In Bill Watterson's comic strip, which ran weekly for a decade, Calvin's parents are excluded by definition from their son's backyard swashbuckling. Whenever Calvin's mother or father are present in one of the comic's frames, Hobbes the tiger is nothing but a stuffed animal. In order for Hobbes to come to life—in order for *Calvin* to come to life, and go careening down the hill without brakes and with a real-life tiger—Calvin's parents need to be, literally, out of the picture.

"This is your *child's* journey," the college admissions counselor advised us from the stage that evening. "Have faith that with our support, your child has got this. And then, please—let your child lead." She stopped to raise an eyebrow. "Trust me—you don't want to be *that* kind of parent."

Everyone in the auditorium chortled. Ho ho, no! Of *course* we weren't those sorts of parents! None of *us* were those nightmare types you heard about, hovering and snowplowing, Varsity-Bluesing their way to racketeering charges. Viewing their children's college acceptances as some sick reflection of themselves. Ha, no! We weren't anything like those other, very bad parents. We were just here to jot down some dates and deadlines. Here to ask for some clarifying details about this process our kids were about to undergo, one that seemed both kind of confusing and also pretty important.

"Should my child take the SAT or the ACT?" one parent asked.

"These days students can take both. Or neither! It's really different for each kid."

"Should students apply early decision?"

"That's a determination each family has to make individually."

"How should a student make their list of colleges?"

"Well, they can start by visiting the schools that seem interesting to them."

We parents began casting sidelong glances at one another. We were being told both to back off and that it was up to us to figure out which tests our students were supposed to take, how they'd apply, and when in our family calendars to visit a long list of schools—a list that would also be up to us to create. Or, excuse me, up to our *children*. But based on what set of criteria? And who else were the students going to look to for support in all of this but their parents?

Before sending us out into the evening more stressed about this process than we had been when we had arrived, the college counselor offered this valediction: "You know, I hear a lot of parents at this stage say 'we.' '*We're* applying to Princeton.' '*We're* applying to MIT.' And I would just like you to consider, as you go home tonight, whether that 'we' can be replaced by 'they.' Please keep that top of mind. This is your child's journey."

Thus begins the rite of passage millions of parents of rising high-school seniors endure each year, bookending the journeys that began when those same children first crossed their doorsteps in carefully chosen infant car seats. And it's quite a closing act. Before a child leaves home for college, a parent must perform what feels like the most momentous act of service for that child they have completed to date: helping them find a place where they can gain acceptance and then stand a chance of decent happiness as they begin their adult lives.

It can be particularly jarring to realize the schools you've been secretly considering as your child's fallback options have become harder to get into than the hard schools used to be. In the early 1990s, my alma mater, Yale University, had about thirteen thousand applicants per year. About twenty-four hundred of them received fat admissions envelopes. When my own fell through our mail slot, it felt both as thrilling and as unlikely as a golden ticket from Willy Wonka himself. Last year more than fifty thousand students applied to Yale; less than four percent of them were accepted. If I look for a college where my kid has the same chance of being accepted today as I did when I applied to Yale—with an acceptance rate of eighteen percent—the closest match is the University of Miami. Which is not to say there's anything less-than about University of Miami; students on Niche.com give it an A+ both for academics and for its "Party Scene," a combination more young people really ought to consider. The point is that the modern valedictorian, with eight AP courses, travel lacrosse schedule, and untold service hours, would be extremely lucky to achieve admission there, only to then face the bewilderment of every nosy grown-up not up to date on admissions statistics when she says she's not going to Harvard.

Once your child embarks on the college application process, you realize telling parents to back off is truly preposterous. Let your child lead the process, while they are also taking Advanced Calculus AB and Spanish IV and playing a sport and creating a nonprofit about which they can craft a moving essay regarding a period of personal growth! Let them be in charge of observing the deadlines of application requirements, while understanding that each one bears no relation to the documents or timelines of the dozen other schools on their list! Let your child lead, while you remain nothing but the facilitator, password manager, sounding board, and whipping boy for the entire enterprise! Let your child handle this thing and the other thing and that form—no, not that form, the one they need to print out because you heard that an email went out, just to the students, that said it was supposed to be on their teachers' desks by 11:59 a.m. yesterday. Yes, you already emailed them the form again. Yes, they should check their inbox, because you definitely sent it.

The system is designed to confound. Are schools really "test-optional"? Really "need-blind"? When a school says they're not tracking interest, should your kid still be clicking on every link that school emails them just in case? The mass confusion is not the fault of college counselors, who usually have a hundred or more high school seniors to guide, students they probably first met about six months ago and now have to write specific and glowing prose about. I suppose it's partly the colleges' fault for being so nonspecific about their expectations and requirements. But who can blame colleges for making their application processes ever more onerous and opaque, in the hopes that the number of applications they have to read won't double again next year?

It is definitely not the parents' fault, but as in so many other arenas, if something has to change, but that change would be really complicated, "let's just make parents feel bad about it" becomes the primary solution. If a parent—and in my admittedly less-than-comprehensive demographic sampling, the mother—does work that is both unpaid and invisible to those not engaged in it, then those standing outside the process can tell themselves that it just cannot be that intensive or hard. Any parent who says it is must be exaggerating. Any parent who says it twice needs to be reminded that all final transcript request forms need to be submitted as hard copies no later than five p.m. today in order for the high school to be willing to submit the student's transcripts at all, and without transcripts the colleges will reject those applications without even reading them, and also, just to reiterate, it is your child's journey.

Any parent who supports her child's byzantine application process with four spreadsheets and eleven open browser tabs ends up ridiculed by society for the work she is doing even while she's fairly certain it could not happen otherwise. It's another moment in which women have to suffer the eyerolls of others for being so terribly extra—the mom version of being a Bridezilla—only this time on behalf of our children, with stakes that feel far higher than the shipping status of two hundred customized napkin rings.

The "*Relax*, Mom" messaging is not even consistently delivered. Year after year college counselors break the news to untold numbers of dismayed families that their hopeful rising senior's last three years of five hours' sleep a night have afforded them the opportunity to get into the University of East Mediocre. If they're lucky. College counselors tend to overcorrect in these conversations, but of course they do—if your kid *does* get into a school deemed to be a reach, they can then say they always had a good feeling about it, while the downside to getting students' hopes up is obviously considerable. Unfortunately, the end result is to make it sound like a kid might not get in anywhere at all, freaking out the same parents they just told to chill out.

While your child's classmates' parents are no doubt going similarly berserk a few blocks away, it's unseemly to discuss the tension while the Hunger Games are still in process. This silence further intensifies the issue. Kids and parents don't talk about the stress of it all with those who would most understand—the other kids and parents going through it—until it's all over. Talking about it would acknowledge that our kids are in competition. Talking about it would highlight the class differences and learning differences it usually feels politer to ignore, although the final results may make those things plain enough. It's like the fourth grade science fair, when it's apparent that the kid who won the blue ribbon had a trifold poster board hand-lettered by her parent. Who also works at a planetarium. It's unfair, but it's too late to do anything about it.

The only people who do want to talk about it are the parents who have just completed the process, thus entering a brief town-crier stage in which they make everyone around them—particularly the parents next in line for this particular ride—aware that it's a "total bloodbath," and that those parents' kids getting in to any college at all has become mere millimeters from impossible. Perhaps not what that next set of parents most need to hear two weeks after they have received their own Calvin and Hobbes binders, and have resolved, no matter what, to keep their children's own admissions processes super-low-key and mellow.

The final intensifying factor in this transitional phase is your own child, suddenly a nest-soiler extraordinaire. The powder keg of tension that is a child's last year at home is, of course, developmentally appropriate. An adolescent psychologically prepares to leave home by becoming increasingly disgusted with their family unit and how tiresome all its members are, the matriarch in particular. An adolescent in this stage is strongly inclined to disagree with any suggestion his mother might make simply because she's the one suggesting it. A broken-down plan for the seventeen essays ahead? A *calendaring session*? Are you *actually serious*, Mom? They're mad at us for creating the spreadsheets. They're mad at us for making them go through any of this at all.

That we cannot convince said children that our efforts on their behalf are born out of love, and not the joy of causing them exasperation, is why college counselors are not all wrong with their backing-off advice. In an ideal world, parents should not be running their children's college admissions sports books from their kitchen tables. If a parent has a child who can manage the process while also eating and sleeping and keeping up with their research for the peer-reviewed journal they're hoping to publish in before applications are due—plus the half-dozen other extracurriculars they're juggling in order to complete all ten activity blanks on the Common Application—that parent should definitely let that child do so.

And yes, a lot of us handled our own college applications processes back in the day just fine. Then again, we handled almost everything ourselves back then. But every step of the college process was different. I picked a handful of schools based on what acting programs my drama teacher said were good, visited none before applying, and finalized my list after the briefest perusal of the brochures I received in the mail. I took the SATs without any preparation. I typed my personal statement in a single Wite-Outed draft on my grandmother's electric typewriter. My essay was about the many definitions of me, and I explained in my first and only draft that I loved Twizzlers but hated the words "these are the best years of your life." I licked the envelopes, hit the mailbox at the corner, and didn't think about any of it again until the acceptance letters started showing up one day after school. Even that felt like a pleasant surprise, a springtime interruption of my focused planning for what really mattered: the skit I'd be doing for Senior Class Day.

Applying to college is nothing like that now. There are of course plenty of kids still handling the process without any adult guidance, but no one would argue that that is to their advantage. That it's become so much more difficult, so much more complicated, and so much more likely to end in a seventeen-year-old's crushing disappointment is not the fault of the parent. Neither is it the fault of a kid who really does his best but regularly leaves his school ID at home in the pants he wore the day before. A kid who does pretty much everything else right, while also doing more hours of homework in a night than his mother used to have in a week.

There may have been some well-meaning but misleading guidance imparted to those kids along the way: that juniors should take the most—and hardest—classes that they can handle. That sophomores should stuff their schedules with far more extracurriculars than is rational. That if students supremely overdeliver for four years of high school, there will be a final commensurate reward: admission to the fanciest schools of their choice, which will never expect those students' families to pay more than they are able—these schools meet one hundred percent of demonstrated need! Then these students and their parents arrive at senior year to find out none of that was quite exactly true, especially when the rules have changed yet again.

Just as I completed writing this essay, the Supreme Court ruled that colleges and universities could no longer specifically consider an applicant's race in their admissions decisions, effectively ending affirmative action as it had existed for decades. Black and brown and AAPI kids will no longer be able to mention their race in their applications, except where they can, because mentioning one's race in an essay will still be acceptable, except in cases where it is not. No one seems very sure how anyone will be able to tell the difference between abiding by the new rule and breaking it. Schools will be responsible for enforcing their compliance with this ruling, not by proving they are taking particular actions, but by proving they are not. But how else will a university be able to demonstrate it is *not* considering students' racial identity during its admission process, if not by decreasing the numbers of non-white students it grants admission?

While no one would argue that the college admissions system was perfect as it was, this decision has overturned a practice meant to correct that system's most historical and central unfairness—granting the gift of higher education primarily to wealthy white students, and males at that—without putting any plausible or actionable alternative in place. Plenty of other levers of admissions preference are still available to be deployed, but students who lack support or knowledge or access or privilege—the students whom affirmative action was intended to benefit—will remain just as unable to parlay years of fencing lessons into a look from a Division III coach as they always have been.

Then there's the new digital SAT, its third overhaul in the last decade, which experts predict will make the test either much easier or much harder. Then there are the FAFSA forms for financial aid, a process the Department of Education set out to simplify and instead made infinitely more complicated. Then there's the advent of AI chatbots, which will either increase the value of writing in one's own, unique voice or make personal statements quickly obsolete. There is only one thing we can count on: the entire admissions process will continue to become even more confusing than it already was. No one seems particularly concerned, though, because any increased turmoil can continue to be blamed on the aggravating, uptight rage of the parents whose kids are currently applying. No need to fix a broken system.

And so we parents will continue to do what we can. We smile into myriad online information sessions. We attempt to right-size our children's goals and dreams in advance. We tell our children they shouldn't worry, that they would be happy at all kinds of schools, which is certainly the case. Then, because it's the best way to optimize their chances of admission, we ask them to choose a single "Early Decision" school, to commit to

Cherish Every Moment

wanting that one outcome the very most. And just when our kids are the most stressed, just when we're most questioning the inequities and confusions of the entire system—and considering how some students must navigate it without any support at all—someone will crack a joke about how it's the overbearing, overthinking parents who have ruined the whole process. And we'll laugh along, swallowing our unease, along with the knowledge that the whole undertaking is unreasonable, arbitrary, and unfair.

We can't fix this with our mindsets, although we can certainly make it worse. We have to prepare our children to leave us, even though both we and our children have mixed feelings about that, which is why we parents have to carefully titrate our involvement. Not too much, not too little.

Sports psychologist Larry Lauer, who advises parents of young elite tennis players on the amount of training and pressure their kids can handle, calls this the "optimal push." Push a prodigy too little and she'll never meet her own full potential. Push too hard, and she might get injured—or just burned out. Lauer says the optimal push isn't one-approach-fits-all; it varies for each child. What is universal? Kids are optimally supported when they believe their parents' love is not contingent on their performance. In order for a child to succeed—whether on the USTA tour or in the Thunderdome of college admissions—a parent's love and support must be unconditional.

Of course it is! I think when I read Lauer's words. Of course my love is unconditional. I support and love my child, no matter what happens. My child knew that.

Of course my child knew that. Look at all these spreadsheets! Didn't he?

HAPPY TO HELP

In the world of Calvin and Hobbes there is not much detail about how Calvin's little life is enabled. How Calvin's father earns money is never specified. Neither is where Calvin's mother shops for all his red striped shirts. Bill Watterson never even gave Calvin's parents names—they remain only "Mom" and "Dad." Calvin's safety and basic happiness are just sort of there, and he is a little boy so secure in the belief that his needs will be met that he has the mental space he needs to create fictional jungles and Martian canyons, horizons offering more adventurous thrills of unpredictability. It's not that Calvin is ungrateful for everything his mother does for him. It's that he never stops to think about it at all, which proves him to be just as he should be: a child who feels safe in his mother's love.

As I prepared to leave my own childhood home for my first year of college, I exhibited a similar lack of curiosity about the things my own mother had done to enable each day of my life. Whether my mother would still love me when I was gone was the last thing on my mind, which was why I spent the last night before my parents drove me to New Haven hanging out with a lifeguard eight months my junior who drove a Mustang convertible.

I still remember being surprised by my mother's disappointment. "But—I told Nana you and I would take a ride up to see her!" she said. Why would I spend my last night at home with the women who raised me when I could spend it with a boy I barely knew who would break up with me a couple of weeks later?

My mother let me go out that night. Two days later—my eighteenth birthday—as we stood outside my freshman dorm and said goodbye, I couldn't understand why my mother was crying. "Don't worry, Mom! I'm going to be fine!" I laughed, as if concern for my well-being was what her tears were about. She didn't have to be sad! I felt completely prepared to need nothing further from her.

Developmental psychologist Laurence Steinberg suggests that what we call a "midlife crisis" is usually caused not by a parent's chronological age, but by her child's stage of life. Among the parents he studied, the storm-and-stress stage nearly always happened while their children were teenagers—whether those parents were in their early forties, as my mother was when I left for college, or a decade older than that, as I am now. For mothers in particular, Steinberg suggests it can be the emptying nest that serves as the moment of crisis, far more than the empty one.

A creeping dread of what was about to happen next hung over me as I consulted my oldest child through his process of leaving home. *You're going to have to let go pretty soon, Mom, and it's going to be rough!* Would I find the coming separation painful? Would my own life change as much as my child's was about to? As it turned out, my relationship with my college-bound senior, and then his younger brother as well, became far more peaceful once the college applications were behind us, my kids on the downhill side of senior year, them rushing toward Class Day and the prom and the pasta dinner while I stood around with all the other mothers saying, again and again, that we didn't know where the time went. We parents were the ones taking teary-eyed photos at our children's graduations, because we remembered all the days that were gone and behind us, because we understood how this moment would become a long-ago memory too.

The only place our kids were looking was forward.

HAPPY TO HELP

The day we dropped my oldest child off at college, two dozen sophomores descended on our SUV at exactly 1:50 p.m., our appointed arrival time. They pulled the boxes and bags and laundry baskets out of the back of our car, shouting the lyrics of whatever song was playing on some wireless speaker nearby, running everything up the four flights of stairs to our son's new room before my husband and I even had our seatbelts unbuckled. My son and his roommate, who recognized each other from their Instagram feeds, embraced at first sight as if they were already the great friends they would quickly become.

I had thought helping my child unpack and get settled would take all afternoon. Sure, I'd be a little sad, but it would give all of us time to adjust. It took about twenty-five minutes, and that included a crash course for my son and his roommate on how fitted sheets worked. Then it was clearly time for my husband and me to leave, not only because four people in a first-year double is a crowd, but also because there wasn't anything left for Mom to do.

There was no time to savor how my child's hard work (and, yes, quietly, in the background, let's say it, my own) had led to this moment. Just the ride on the shuttle bus back to the parking area so my husband and I could begin our ten-hour drive home without him. Our son came along with us for that ride, either because he was unsure about what he'd be doing next, or maybe because he thought his mother might like that.

He hugged us goodbye on the sidewalk, first his father, then me.

Don't let go, I thought. *Not quite yet.*

Okay. Now.

I watched my son reboard the shuttle bus, watched him through the window frame as he chose a seat and then rode away looking at his phone instead of waving goodbye. It was exactly as it should be, his next adventure beginning once Mom was out of the picture, when Mom couldn't see him any longer.

It Has to Be You

When my daughter was in third grade she got a headache that would not go away. It was not there, and then all of a sudden it was, although when I looked back it had been predicting its own arrival for some time.

For the past two years she had been telling me her stomach hurt so often that I stopped hearing it. She couldn't have a stomachache *every day*. Not with her consistently sunny personality. Not the way she was running around. But when she mentioned the nausea and pain at her next checkup—and I sheepishly confirmed that, come to think of it, she had been talking about it for months—the pediatrician referred her to a specialist. When that gastroenterologist ran a series of tests and couldn't find anything, we privately conferred and agreed it might just be a case of mild anxiety. That was the simplest and most likely explanation, although my child had never seemed particularly anxious to me. At the time none of the other things that happened to my daughter had happened yet. At the time I didn't know there was something called abdominal migraine. Since the GI was not a neurologist, she never considered it either.

Then my daughter started mentioning being dizzy. One day as I walked her to school she stopped right in the middle of the sidewalk. "I feel like I'm on a roller coaster," she said. I was briefly alarmed; it passed after about thirty seconds; we kept walking. Then a few weeks later she woke up feeling dizzy even while sitting down. An hour later the headache began. That night our babysitter called me at my friend's wedding reception, interrupting my shouted conversation at the bar, to tell me I needed to come home right away.

Three weeks later, after twenty-one days of reassuring my child that she would surely wake up feeling much better, her migraine had still not broken. The pain, nausea, and dizziness had swirled into a constant locked state preventing my child from doing almost anything at all. Her pediatrician sent us to the emergency room for a "migraine cocktail," a combination of IV drugs that usually provide quick relief. But eighteen hours and two of those cocktails later, nothing had changed, and the buzzing lights and constant beeping of the machines were driving my child increasingly mad.

The attending physician, reviewing my child's chart after the second IV treatment proved unsuccessful, was considering whether to admit her to the pediatric ward. He checked through the usual with me: the patient's height and weight, was my pregnancy with her full-term, all those back-to-the-beginning questions that seem designed to work the last nerves of frazzled parents. Then he asked me something else.

"Does your daughter have a type A personality?"

I stared at him, then at my child, curled in the hiked-up hospital bed, shoulders up to her ears in a futile attempt to block out all the lights and sounds, including the wailing of another patient somewhere down the hall. "She's eight years old," I answered. Seriously, was this guy insane?

"Well. I just meant, does she get really rigid about her schoolwork? Or her surroundings?"

This time I considered the question more carefully. Was my child type A? While I had shrugged at anxiety as the probable explanation of her chronic stomach pain two years earlier, was it true? And if so, how else had I seen it manifest?

After spending most of the last three weeks in bed, my child had indeed come to prefer her nightstand prescriptions and supplements lined up to face the front. Even before that, when she was too nauseated or dizzy to play with friends, she spent time alone in her room creating flawless miniature worlds for her American Girl dolls, perfect reproductions of airplane cabins and smoothie shops. As my child's pain had increased, so had her efforts to control the few small things she could. But her feeling sick was to blame for those sad and futile efforts at creating order. Not the other way around.

"It is not my child's fault she is in pain," I told the doctor. "And we're not going to tell ourselves that it is just so we can stop looking for what is really wrong."

I climbed into my child's bed and put my arms around her until he went away. We didn't see that doctor after that.

After we got home from the hospital a few days later I began researching how to help my daughter, whose migraine was "maybe sometimes a little better" but which still had not broken. The rigid "migraine personality," as defined in the 1930s by Harold Wolff, was only a little better than the previously prevailing belief that people with migraines were hysterical, exaggerating, or both. Wolff explained that the migraine personality "aims to gain approval by doing more and better," creating "a system of excellent performance even at high cost of energy." Crippling headaches were the inevitable result, unless that system of excellent performance could be overthrown. Since that was up to the person with the migraine, her doctor could do little but wish her the very best.

While the migraine personality has long been disproven, the true causes of migraine have proven trickier to unravel, and the resulting pain is suffered far more frequently by women. It is therefore still widely assumed that a female patient's migraine must arise, at least in part, from her own disposition. Joan Didion, herself a lifelong migraine sufferer, wrote about her frustration at the presumption that people with migraines "are making ourselves sick, that we bring it on ourselves." Even so, when Didion's doctor mused that her "messy hair" didn't exactly fit the migraine personality profile—and then asked whether she was a "compulsive housekeeper"—Didion rejected those old saws of perfectionism while still accepting the diagnosis. "The doctor was right nonetheless," she wrote. "Perfection can also take the form of spending most of a week writing and rewriting and not writing a single paragraph."

Sociologist Joanna Kempner has highlighted Didion's acceptance of self-blame in this case as a common human instinct. She writes that we internalize the ways others classify us. We adapt our behavior and senses of self to how others perceive us. If I am told that I am the sort of person who is always happy to help, I probably will be. If I have a migraine, and you tell me people with migraines are type A, then my sense of self will come to include that assessment, whether or not it is really so. And when even someone as acutely observant as Didion was susceptible, what hope is there for the rest of us? How are any of us, migraine sufferers or just women with too much to do, supposed to reject these perceptions rather than shape our identities around them?

Today scientists pinpoint neurobiological processes as the true cause of migraine. Estrogen is an aggravating factor, which probably explains why migraine sufferers are predominantly female. But it's still widely presumed that the nervous and tense chicken lays the migraine egg. And it remains a slippery slope from "people who have migraine attacks—who are almost all female—sometimes also exhibit rigidity" to "Lady, your headaches might go away if you stopped being such a tight-ass."

I lay there in the emergency room with my suffering daughter, resisting the urge to kiss her on the back of the head because even that would hurt. I lay there furious that a medical professional would even consider blaming a child for her own pain. Then I recognized it as just another version of the suggestions that I had, ever since I was about my daughter's age, either accepted as flaws in myself to fix or rejected angrily without knowing how else I might change what was happening.

That I made things harder than they had to be.

That I created difficulty and pain instead of choosing not to worry.

That I overcompensated because I thought everything had to be perfect.

That my unnecessarily high standards needed to be checked, lest they be unpleasant for those around me.

I had folded all these things into my sense of self. Now I saw that my daughter would be receiving those same messages.

And that she had already. From me.

My daughter had always been a kid who cried a lot over minor bumps and scrapes. She spoke of small discomforts, then went right back to playing with her friends, which made me think whatever she had been complaining about couldn't really have hurt as much as she said it did. As her reports of pain increased, as she stopped on the walk to school because she was too dizzy to keep going, there was still a small part of me that believed she had to be exaggerating.

I told her she was a big girl, that she could certainly make it the rest of the way.

I told her she was fine when she knew that she was not.

This is exactly what I thought I was supposed to do as her parent, but the pain was winning now, having grown over time until a well-meaning mother could not ignore it, until the emergency room was out of ideas. It was long past time for me to listen.

Much later, I would hear a pain specialist explain that children who make big fusses over seemingly small injuries are usually not overly sensitive. Rather, they're experts at pain management. They are, in fact, better at it than the rest of us.

My child was particularly strong. Especially when she told me she needed help and I didn't really listen. That she had to work so hard to make her struggle visible, even to her mother, meant she was also very brave.

The same can be said for anyone who struggles.

The same can be said for ourselves.

When we are in difficult seasons of life, they are hard because they are hard, not because there's something wrong with us. They are hard because they are real, not because we make them harder on purpose. And if others don't always perceive us as struggling, it's because we've become quite capable of handling more than should be expected.

Our labor as women, both practical and emotional, is something the world assumes is an endlessly renewable resource, continuously available in whatever amounts might be required. Pretending we can handle it all can't be the way to live the rest of our lives. Being good at juggling only means we will get handed more balls. Taking care of the ones we love doesn't have to mean absorbing every body blow for them. But our worlds around us are often structured assuming that we will, so it is up to us to figure out when that's not serving us, or the situation, or maybe both.

When I'm struggling, I don't want someone to tell me to look on the bright side. I want someone to tell me that I am courageous, even when I doubt myself. Above all, I want someone to tell me that what I'm handling is absolutely nuts. Otherwise the doubt reflected back by the world will keep me second-guessing and self-blaming on top of the actual burdens I carry. Otherwise I keep accepting suggestions to change myself, even though those prescriptions may be the very things that are keeping me stuck.

As long as we put the expectations on ourselves both to do more than we can handle and to fix our own feelings about that, nothing much will change. Accepting it's not our fault things are hard is a lot like a person with migraine accepting it's not her fault she's in pain. It doesn't mean she stops doing anything to control the attacks, or that none of those things might sometimes work. But guilt rarely lightens the load.

I hope that my daughter won't take on more than she is able. I hope she will not falter when others tell her that what she's experiencing is all in her head. I hope she will be better able to push back on those narratives when they occur, even if they come from the sort of people she's supposed to obey.

My daughter's migraine disorder has become more manageable since that day in the emergency room, not because of an attitude adjustment, but because of time and proper treatment. She takes daily medication that raises her migraine threshold, so that when unpredictable and uncontrollable events occur—a sudden drop in barometric pressure, a jackhammer outside the window—debilitating pain is less likely to result. She also stops and rests at the first sign of trouble. She doesn't keep going until she wakes up burned.

One day during seventh-grade gym class, while doing sprints with the rest of her class, she felt the room spinning, recognized the vertigo as her first sign of an oncoming migraine, and sat down at the edge of the gym to rest.

A PE teacher who was new to the school told my child to get up and rejoin the activity, likely thinking she was doing my daughter a favor, not allowing her to play fainting-couch. Insisting that she push through, preventing her from playing small. "I've never heard of children getting migraines," this teacher said when my child tried to explain. "You need to get up right now."

And here is where my daughter did what I would never have entitled myself to do at her age. She stayed right where she was. "I need to sit here until class is over," she replied. "Check my chart. That's what it says. If you don't believe me, you can call my mom."

That teacher did check her chart. And then she did call me, to wholeheartedly apologize, first to me, then to my child.

It Has to Be You

Maybe my daughter will be able to say no even when someone tells her she is required to raise her hand. Maybe she will allow herself to walk away from those Trixie La Boom Boom situations that are just never, ever going to work. But there will probably be other times my child will be asked to give more than she should. At those times I hope she gives herself some slack. I hope she gives herself self-compassion when she does her very best only to find that it will never be enough.

―――

Not so long ago I was on a Zoom call with ten or so people I care about, in the disembodied Brady Bunch format that had come to seem normal thanks to the pandemic's enforced separations. It was the first time this group had gathered in this particular way, although our topic was familiar. Our loved one's struggles with addiction had returned. So had our own struggles with it.

I had hoped that if one dropped the rope, that meant the things held too tightly could be permanently set free. But deciding you're not going to worry about something anymore doesn't always mean that problem will magically resolve. Sometimes our problems stay there in the corner of the room. All we can do then is make friends.

On other calls like this I might have donned my armor, taken up the spear, and told everyone what to do next. *This Way to the Solution!*

But this time I did not raise my hand, because none of that had ever been the answer.

This time I did not raise my hand, even though I really did know the answer.

The answer was that we were powerless.

And all we needed to do was listen.

One of the other members of our group had found an outside professional to guide our discussion. For the last hour she had listened patiently to us all. Then she told us what she thought. "I really think," she said, "that if anyone is going to make this happen, it's going to be you, Amy. It has to be you."

I stared at the little square of this stranger on my laptop screen, next to the square of myself reflecting back at me. How had she read that dynamic so quickly? Why did it seem so completely obvious?

Was this idea—that it had to be me—the actual truth, after everything I had done to convince myself it wasn't?

Maybe I just needed to work harder. Maybe there was one more thing I hadn't tried.

Maybe she was right: it had to be me, and now was exactly the wrong time to give up.

"Don't say that to me," I said, surprised at my anger, maybe at her, maybe at the tears that were springing to my eyes.

"No, I do. I really believe in you!" this stranger said, mistaking my distress for something that required only a little extra encouragement. "I *know* you can do it. Tell her, everyone."

"I am asking you," I said again. "Please. *Don't say that.*" I covered my face, too ashamed to watch a tiny version of myself falling apart.

I knew I was not supposed to be able to do what she was asking. I knew that it was absolutely wrong of her to ask. I still wished, above all, that I could.

I could hear the confusion in the stranger's voice as she stammered an apology. I could feel the rest of the group there in their own little squares, looking on in silence. We all stayed there, suspended in our separate living room realities, unsure of what was supposed to happen next.

"I choose not to" is an uncomfortable place to live. When the world tells overcompensating women we need to be brave enough to say "no"—either because we really can't say "yes" or just because we don't want to—the world forgets that the first hard part is the silence that may follow. People aren't going to stop asking us to do things we can't or shouldn't. Saying "no" is just the first step in an extended dance of renegotiation with partners who, whether they're disincentivized or just baffled, are unprepared to respond.

It's hard for those of us who have often rushed to fill that silence to just sit in it, not to end it by raising our hands. To let the silence exist before moving forward into something unknown. It's far easier for us to fall back into the familiarity of the way things were before, of the way things may have been for as long as we can remember.

When I was about the same age my daughter is now, bidding farewell to my diary with a to-do list for my future, the final task I assigned myself was extraordinarily open-ended:

Do everything I can to make the people I really love happy.

I didn't vow to make people I love "really happy"; I promised to strive constantly for the happiness of the ones I "really loved." Maybe I inadvertently garbled my word order. And maybe what

HAPPY TO HELP

I wrote is exactly what my grandiose adolescent self intended: I would help the people I cared about most by rescuing them from anything resembling sorrow or pain. And once I delivered them happiness, it would serve as proof that they were the ones who had mattered most.

But prove to whom? And who exactly had asked me to make that happen? I can "really love" people without making them happy. Those people never expected me to guarantee them happiness in the first place. And those people get to be loved by me no matter what their emotional states are, no matter what they're struggling with. It was never mine to ensure that the perfect peace and happiness of my loved ones was achieved. Forever fixing our loved ones' lives isn't the point. Our job is to love them while they suffer.

Our job is to love ourselves, even when we can't fix what is wrong.

Even when *we* are what is wrong.

Who might I become if I choose no longer to carry those burdens?

Who might I become if I accept that the people I really love will be there for me, even when I am the one asking for help?

Who might I become if I let myself be seen at my most frustrated, and failed, and sad?

The hardest part of letting go might be the getting ready. It's harder to worry about what will happen if we let go than to live in the moments just after we have.

I sat there on that Zoom call with my loved ones in the weird silence that comes after it becomes clear that something new and different is taking place.

They all stayed there with me while my heart cracked open.

No one told me it was wrong or silly to feel how I felt. No one handed me a solution; there wasn't any. We sat there in silence in our little squares, separate and together, in relationship through a hard situation.

We can't just sit here and do nothing, I found myself thinking as I sobbed.

But yes, we can. Our presence together is enough, there among the scattered pieces with instructions that are confusing and don't work. They never will. They never did.

We are worthy even when we are unsure, when we sit together with things that are imperfect and broken and hard, between the inhale and the exhale, in the moment just before something else happens next.

NOTES ON SOURCES

I am grateful for having been granted the following permissions:

From the estate of Lois Duncan, authorization to include the entire text of "The Oldest Sister" from Duncan's poetry collection *Seasons of the Heart*—a poem that I could recite from memory forty years after my mother gave it to me.

From Rose Cook, who allowed me to excerpt "A Poem for Someone Who is Juggling Her Life" from her poetry collection *Notes from a Bright Field* (Cultured Llama Publishing, 2013) as this book's epigraph—summing up most of what I learned during the years described in this book in just a few powerful lines.

I really do love research and want to acknowledge all the other authors and scientists and scholars whose work I highlighted and reread while writing this book, and whose ideas provided many light-bulb moments along the way.

For my essays that touch on perceptions of gender, motherhood, and the invisible workload, I drew insight from Darcy Lockman's book *All the Rage*, Deborah Levy's memoir *The Cost of Living*, Allison Daminger's study "Thinking Gender: The Cognitive Dimension of Household Labor," and Natalia Imperatori-Lee's notion of "mourning rituals."

For my essays on the adolescent psyche, I am indebted to the work of the psychologists Dr. Lisa Damour and Dr. Nancy Darling on teen/parent conflict, Dr. David Elkind's research on egocentrism in adolescence, Dr. Larry Lauer's notion of the "optimal push," and Dr. Laurence Steinberg's book *Crossing Paths*.

For my essay on multitasking, sociology professor Leah Ruppanner's writing and research led me to the experiments of Dr. Patricia Hirsch and Dr. Iring Koch, and from there to an earlier study performed by Dr. Gijsbert Stoet and others. My explanation of an "extinction burst" is based on that of Dr. James Linder.

For my essay on productivity, I was inspired by Tonianne DeMaria Barry and Jim Benson's *Personal Kanban*, Oliver Burkeman's *Four Thousand Weeks*, and Gretchen Rubin's *Outer Order, Inner Calm*.

As part of my discussions of the "migraine brain" and of perfectionism, I have included quotes from Joan Didion's essay "In Bed" and Dr. Harold Wolff's manual *Headache and Other Head Pain*, both of which were first introduced to me by Joanna Kempner's book *Not Tonight: Migraine and the Politics of Gender and Health*. I am also indebted to the perfectionism research of Dr. Paul L. Hewitt and Dr. Gordon L. Flett.

I relied upon Dr. James Dickinson's explanation of "zebras" in medicine and the fourth edition of *Developmental-Behavioral Pediatrics*' description of Munchausen syndrome by proxy in my own references to these terms.

For my essays about the pandemic and its many insidious effects, I refer to Ed Yong and his Pulitzer Prize–winning explanatory reporting on long Covid in *The Atlantic*; Dr. Ghasem Rahmatpour Rokni and Dr. Sung Ha Lim's research on the relationship between COVID-19 and vitiligo; and Dr. Marlee Bower's research on the loneliness that resulted from isolation.

Notes on Sources

For my thoughts on peacefulness and acceptance, I am thankful for Mihaly Csikszentmihalyi's *Flow: The Psychology of Optimal Experience*, cultural theorist Meredith Jones's concept of "stretched middle age," and psychologist John Wearden's explanation of Paul Janet's philosophy of subjective time.

Finally, I am grateful for all the texts that shaped a young voracious reader, for better and otherwise: *Go Ask Alice*, Laura Ingalls Wilder's *Little House on the Prairie*, Peg Bracken's *The I Hate to Cook Book*, countless issues of *Young Miss* magazine, and all those Erma Bombeck columns my mother taped to our refrigerator.

ACKNOWLEDGMENTS

First, my profound thanks to Andrea Robinson, whose wise and rigorous editing improved this book immeasurably. Thanks also to Kathleen Harris, who helped me further sharpen the focus of these pages; to Gillian McNamara, my brilliant and always-supportive agent; and to Zibby Owens, who told me I should write another book and then gave me the incredible opportunity to do so.

Special thanks to everyone at Zibby Books: Anne Messitte, Bridie Loverro, Gabriela Capasso, Diana Tramontano, Jordan Blumetti, Chelsea Grogan, Sherri Puzey, and the entire team. Thank you, Sherian Brown, for your thorough copyedits, and thank you, Abby Weintraub, for your truly beautiful cover design.

I am indebted to the input of these creative partners on earlier versions of some of the material in these pages: Julie Kramer, who first helped me find the stories that mattered in my eighth-grade diary; Kerry Sparks, who edited an earlier version of "Never Give Up"; and Ann Imig, who edited an essay about the same events that later became the basis for "First, Do No Harm."

Many thanks to the early readers of this book, whose thoughtful feedback and support were crucial to its completion: Kathleen Furin, Nancy Davis Kho, Mollie Wilson O'Reilly, Margaret Ables, Julie Kramer, Ann Spence, Cece Heraty, Mary Laura Philpott, Gretchen Rubin, and Daria Colombo.

Acknowledgments

Thank you to my writer friends who offered BTDT encouragement and advice at every stage of the process: KJ Dell'Antonia, Jennie Nash, Sarina Bowen, Christina Geist, Jessica Lahey, Mimi Lichtenstein, Carla Naumburg, and Laura Vanderkam, as well as all my fellow Zibby Books authors.

Thank you to Christina Hart and Sarah Levithan Daniels, whose assistance gave me more time to write.

Finally, my deepest gratitude to my entire family, especially my parents, my three children, and my beloved husband, David. Thank you for listening to my read-aloud drafts; thank you for buoying me during my crises of confidence; thank you for your generosity of time and spirit that gave me space and made this book possible.

Thank you all for having been happy to help.

ABOUT THE AUTHOR

Amy Wilson is the author of the memoir *When Did I Get Like This?* and the co-host of *What Fresh Hell: Laughing in the Face of Motherhood*, a Webby-honored podcast with hundreds of episodes and more than ten million downloads. Wilson's writing has also appeared in *Real Simple*, *Redbook*, *Parenting*, NPR Books, *Babble*, CNN.com, and *The New York Times*. Wilson is also an actor who has appeared on Broadway, as a series regular on network sitcoms, and as a comedy performer in *Saturday Night Live*'s Studio 8H. She is a proud native of Scranton, Pennsylvania, a graduate of Yale University, and lives with her family in New York City.